3 Days in Bue

MW01206485

Welcome to your three-day guide to **Buenos Aires**, one of the world's top tourist destinations. With millions of visitors each year, this magnificent city offers a wide variety of activities and experiences. This guide is packed with tips, maps, and useful travel information to ensure that you make the most of your time in this bustling metropolis without getting lost.

Thanks to the contributions of local experts, we've included the best insider tips on where to stay, what to do, and what to avoid. Buenos Aires is known for its diverse neighborhoods, and we'll explore the most important ones in this guide, including Palermo, Recoleta, San Telmo, La Boca, and Downtown.

All of the maps provided in this guide are available in online mode through Google Maps, making it easy to navigate your way around the city. We hope that this guide will help you have a fantastic time in Buenos Aires, and thank you for choosing Guidora as your travel guide.

Contents

I. Introduction

A. Overview of Buenos Aires

Welcome to Buenos Aires, the vibrant and cosmopolitan capital of Argentina! Often referred to as the "Paris of South America," Buenos Aires is a unique blend of European architecture, Latin American passion, and a rich cultural history. With a population of over 15 million people in its metropolitan area, the city is the heart of Argentina's political, economic, and cultural life.

Located on the western shore of the Río de la Plata, Buenos Aires is known for its stunning architecture, which features an eclectic mix of styles such as Art Deco, Neoclassical, and Beaux-Arts. The city's numerous parks and green spaces provide a pleasant contrast to its bustling streets and busy neighborhoods.

Buenos Aires is a city that never sleeps, with a lively nightlife scene that includes world-class tango shows, innovative restaurants, and an array of bars and clubs. The city is also home to several renowned museums, art galleries, and theaters, making it a thriving hub for the arts.

As you explore the different neighborhoods of Buenos Aires, you will discover the rich history of the city, from its colonial past to its role as the birthplace of tango. The vibrant street life, friendly locals, and captivating culture make Buenos Aires an unforgettable destination for travelers from all over the world.

In this guide, we will provide you with all the essential information you need to plan your trip to Buenos Aires, including tips on where to stay, how to get around, and what to see and do during your visit. Get ready to fall in love with this enchanting city!

B. A Brief History

Buenos Aires is a city steeped in history, with a rich cultural heritage that spans back centuries. From its founding as a Spanish colony in the 16th century to its present-day status as a vibrant and cosmopolitan metropolis, the history of Buenos Aires is a fascinating story that is well worth exploring.

The **founding** of Buenos Aires can be traced back to **1536**, when Spanish explorer Pedro de Mendoza arrived on the shores of the **Rio de la Plata.** Mendoza established a settlement on the site of present-day Buenos Aires, which he named Nuestra Señora Santa María del Buen Ayre (Our Lady St. Mary of the Good Winds). However, the harsh conditions and conflicts with the indigenous population forced the Spanish to abandon the settlement in 1541.

It wasn't until 1580 that Buenos Aires was officially founded, this time by Juan de Garay, who established a new settlement on the same site. This new settlement was named Ciudad de la Santísima Trinidad y Puerto de Santa María de los Buenos Aires (City of the Most Holy Trinity and Port of Saint Mary of the Good Winds), which was eventually shortened to just Buenos Aires.

Throughout the 17th and 18th centuries, Buenos Aires continued to grow as an important port city, serving as a hub for trade with Spain and other European powers. However, the city's position as a remote outpost of the Spanish empire meant that it was largely cut off from the rest of the world and experienced only slow growth.

It wasn't until the 19th century that Buenos Aires truly began to come into its own. In 1810, the city played a key role in the Argentine War of Independence, which saw Argentina break free from Spanish colonial rule. The city also became a major center of trade, with its port serving as a gateway to South America for goods and immigrants.

During this time, Buenos Aires experienced a period of rapid growth and modernization, with new buildings, infrastructure, and cultural institutions springing up throughout the city. In 1853, the Argentine Constitution was signed in Buenos Aires, laying the foundation for a new democratic government.

Throughout the latter half of the 19th century and into the 20th century, Buenos Aires continued to thrive, with its population swelling and its economy booming. The city became a hub for the arts, with tango music and dance emerging as a uniquely Argentine cultural export.

However, **the 20th century** also brought its share of challenges for Buenos Aires. In the **1930s and 1940s,** political instability and economic turmoil plagued the city, as Argentina struggled to find its footing in a rapidly changing world. During this time, Buenos Aires saw periods of civil unrest and political violence, as well as a wave of immigration from Europe, Asia, and other parts of Latin America.

Despite these challenges, Buenos Aires remained a vibrant and culturally rich city throughout the 20th century. Today, it is one of the largest and most important cities in South America, with a population of over 3 million people. Its rich history and cultural heritage are evident throughout the city, from its historic neighborhoods and buildings to its vibrant arts and culinary scenes.

One of the best ways to explore the history of Buenos Aires is by visiting some of its most iconic landmarks and attractions. For example, the **Plaza de Mayo,** located in the heart of the city, is a historic public square that has played a key role in many of Argentina's most important political and cultural events. The **Casa Rosada,** which overlooks the plaza, is the presidential palace and a symbol of Argentine democracy.

Another must-visit attraction is the **Recoleta Cemetery**, which is home to the graves of many of Buenos Aires' most famous and influential citizens, including **Eva Perón** (the wife of **Argentine President Juan Perón**). The cemetery is also notable for its striking architecture and impressive collection of ornate mausoleums.

In addition to these famous landmarks, Buenos Aires is also home to numerous museums and cultural institutions that provide a deeper insight into the city's history and heritage. The **Museum of Latin American Art of Buenos Aires (MALBA)** is a must-visit for art lovers, with an extensive collection of works from some of the most important artists in the region.

For those interested in Argentine history, the **National Historical Museum** is a fascinating destination, with exhibits on everything from pre-Columbian indigenous cultures to the country's recent political history. The **Museum of Immigration** is also a must-visit, showcasing the experiences of the millions of immigrants who have come to Buenos Aires over the years.

Of course, no exploration of Buenos Aires' history would be complete without a deep dive into the city's vibrant **tango culture**. Tango music and dance originated in Buenos Aires in the late 19th century and have since become one of the city's most famous and beloved cultural exports. Visitors to Buenos Aires can attend tango shows and performances throughout the city, or even take tango lessons themselves.

Today, Buenos Aires is a city that continues to evolve and grow, with a diverse and multicultural population and a thriving economy. Its rich history and cultural heritage are an important part of what makes it such a fascinating and compelling destination for visitors from around the world. Whether you're interested in exploring the city's landmarks and museums, immersing yourself in its vibrant arts and music scenes, or simply strolling through its historic neighborhoods and sampling its culinary delights, there is no shortage of things to see and do in Buenos Aires.

C. Culture and Lifestyle

The culture and lifestyle of Buenos Aires are deeply rooted in its diverse history, which is evident in the city's unique blend of European and Latin American influences. The porteños, as the residents of Buenos Aires are known, are famous for their warmth, passion, and zest for life.

Tango: Tango is synonymous with Buenos Aires, and the city's soul is inextricably linked to this passionate and captivating dance. Born in the late 19th century in the working-class neighborhoods, tango has evolved into a cultural phenomenon that can be seen in the city's many milongas (tango dance halls) and street performances. Visitors can immerse themselves in the world of tango by attending a live show, taking a dance lesson, or simply watching local dancers in the streets.

Gastronomy: The cuisine of Buenos Aires is a reflection of the city's diverse population, with Italian, Spanish, and indigenous influences. Argentina is famous for its high-quality beef, and a visit to a traditional parrilla (steakhouse) is a must. Empanadas, choripán, and milanesa are other popular local dishes. The city's café culture is also a significant aspect of the porteño lifestyle, with historic cafés and confiterías (pastry shops) serving as popular meeting spots for locals.

Arts and Literature: Buenos Aires has a vibrant arts scene, boasting numerous museums, galleries, and theaters that showcase both contemporary and classic works. The city has a rich literary tradition, with many famous writers, such as **Jorge Luis Borges and Julio Cortázar**, calling it home. Bookstores and literary cafés can be found throughout the city, providing ample opportunities for bibliophiles to indulge in their passion.

Sports: Football (soccer) is a national obsession in Argentina, and Buenos Aires is home to some of the country's most famous clubs, such as Boca Juniors and River Plate. Attending a football match is an unforgettable experience, with the fervor of the fans creating an electric atmosphere. Other popular sports in the city include rugby, tennis, and polo.

Festivals and Events: Buenos Aires hosts numerous festivals and events throughout the year, celebrating everything from film and theater to food and music. Some notable events include the Buenos Aires International Film Festival, the International Tango Festival, and the Feria de Mataderos, a weekly cultural fair showcasing traditional Argentine music, dance, and crafts.

The lifestyle of Buenos Aires is characterized by a balance between tradition and modernity, with the city's rich cultural heritage coexisting alongside its thriving contemporary arts scene. The spirited energy and passion of the porteños make Buenos Aires a truly unique and unforgettable destination.

D. Understanding Argentinians

As a traveler to Argentina, understanding the local culture and way of life is essential to making the most of your trip. Argentinians are known for their warmth, hospitality, and passionate nature, but there are also certain customs and cultural nuances that are important to be aware of in order to avoid misunderstandings or offense. Here are some tips and insights to help you better understand Argentinian culture:

Lifestyle and Economy:

Argentinians have a very relaxed and laid-back lifestyle. Family and social relationships are very important, and it is common for people to gather in large groups for meals or social events. Lunch is the main meal of the day, and it is typically eaten around 1 or 2 pm. Dinner is usually eaten later in the evening, often starting around 9 or 10 pm.

Argentina is a middle-income country, with a diverse economy that includes agricultural exports, manufacturing, and tourism. In recent years, the country has experienced periods of economic instability and inflation, but it remains a popular destination for international travelers due to its rich cultural heritage and natural beauty.

Culture and Traditions:

Argentina is a country with a rich cultural heritage, blending indigenous, European, and African influences. The country is particularly famous for its tango music and dance, which originated in the working-class neighborhoods of Buenos Aires in the late 19th century. Tango is still an important part of Argentine culture today, with many tango clubs and dance schools throughout the country.

Argentinians are also known for their love of football (soccer), which is considered a national obsession. The country has produced some of the greatest football players in history, and attending a football match is an exciting and memorable experience for visitors.

Religion is an important part of Argentine culture, with the majority of the population identifying as Roman Catholic. However, the country is also home to a diverse array of religious traditions, including Protestantism, Judaism, and Islam.

Do's and Don'ts:

When interacting with Argentinians, it is important to keep in mind some key cultural customs and norms. Here are some do's and don'ts to keep in mind:

Do:

- Greet people with a handshake or kiss on the cheek (depending on the situation and relationship)
- Dress well and take pride in your appearance.
- Use formal titles (such as "Doctor" or "Professor") when addressing people with advanced degrees or professional titles.
- Be polite and respectful in social situations.

Don't:

- Be overly direct or confrontational in social situations.
- Be late for appointments or social events.
- Interrupt people when they are speaking.
- Touch people without their permission

It is also important to be aware of the potential for cultural misunderstandings or offense. For example, it is considered rude to refuse an invitation to someone's home, as hospitality is an important part of Argentine culture. Similarly, making critical comments about Argentina or its people is likely to be met with offense.

In general, it is best to approach interactions with Argentinians with an open and respectful attitude, and to be willing to learn and adapt to local customs and traditions.

E. Important Argentinian Personalities

Buenos Aires, the vibrant capital of Argentina, is a city that thrives on its rich cultural heritage. This heritage is shaped by a plethora of personalities who have left an indelible mark on the world stage. From the realms of art, culture, sports, music, and movies, these personalities have become synonymous with the Argentine spirit. Here are some of the most influential figures that every visitor to Buenos Aires should know about.

1. Jorge Luis Borges

Jorge Luis Borges, one of the 20th century's most influential writers, was born and raised in Buenos Aires. His works, which blend philosophy, fantasy, and literary gamesmanship, have become classics of world literature. His collections of stories, such as "Ficciones" and "El Aleph," are celebrated for their complex narratives and metaphysical explorations. Borges' influence can be felt throughout Buenos Aires, from the National Library where he once served as director, to the many bookstores and cafes where his spirit lives on.

2. Eva Perón

Eva Perón, affectionately known as Evita, was a charismatic figure who left a lasting impact on Argentine politics and culture. As the First Lady of Argentina, she championed for labor rights and women's suffrage, earning her the love and admiration of the working class. Her life and legacy are immortalized in the Evita Museum, located in the Palermo district of Buenos Aires. The museum, housed in a mansion that was once a shelter for women and children established by the Eva Perón Foundation, offers a glimpse into her extraordinary life.

3. Diego Maradona

Diego Maradona, widely regarded as one of the greatest footballers of all time, is a national icon in Argentina. His skill and flair on the pitch, particularly during the 1986 World Cup, have become the stuff of legend. Maradona played for Boca Juniors, one of Buenos Aires' most famous football clubs, and his influence can be felt throughout the city. The club's stadium, La Bombonera, is a must-visit for any football fan, and a mural of Maradona adorns its exterior, a testament to his enduring legacy.

4. Carlos Gardel

Carlos Gardel is a name synonymous with tango, Argentina's most famous cultural export. Known as "The King of Tango," Gardel was a singer, songwriter, and actor who played a crucial role in popularizing tango internationally. His music is still played in the traditional tango houses, known as 'milongas,' throughout Buenos Aires. A visit to his mausoleum in the Chacarita Cemetery is a pilgrimage for many tango enthusiasts.

5. María de los Remedios Alicia Rodriga Varo y Uranga

Known as Remedios Varo, she was a Spanish surrealist artist who spent her early years in Argentina. Her work, characterized by mystical and fantastical themes, has been influential in the art world. While her paintings are scattered in museums around the world, her influence can be felt in Buenos Aires' thriving art scene, particularly in the city's many galleries and art spaces.

6. Gustavo Cerati

Gustavo Cerati was a singer-songwriter, composer, and producer who is considered one of the most important and influential figures of Ibero-American rock. As the lead singer of the band Soda Stereo, he helped shape the sound of Latin rock and continues to inspire musicians today. His music can be heard in the bars and clubs of Buenos Aires, keeping his legacy alive.

7. Ricardo Darín

Ricardo Darín is one of Argentina's most renowned actors, known for his roles in critically acclaimed films like "The Secret in TheirEyes," "Nine Queens," and "Wild Tales." His performances, marked by their depth and authenticity, have earned him a place among the greats of world cinema. The Argentine cinema scene, particularly in Buenos Aires, is vibrant and diverse, and Darín's influence is palpable. A visit to one of the city's historic cinemas, like the Gaumont or the Lorca, offers a chance to experience this rich cinematic tradition.

8. Marta Minujín

Marta Minujín, a pioneering conceptual and performance artist, is known for her audacious works that often engage with political and social issues. Her most famous work, "The Parthenon of Books," a full-scale replica of the Parthenon made from banned books, was a powerful statement on censorship. Minujín's innovative spirit is reflected in Buenos Aires' contemporary art scene, particularly in institutions like the Museum of Modern Art and the MALBA.

9. Mercedes Sosa

Mercedes Sosa, known as "La Negra," was one of the preeminent figures of the Nueva Canción movement, which combined traditional folk music with political activism. Her powerful voice and poignant lyrics made her a symbol of resistance during Argentina's military dictatorship. Sosa's music continues to resonate in Buenos Aires, where the tradition of politically engaged music is alive and well.

10. Lionel Messi

Lionel Messi, often considered the best footballer in the world, was born in Argentina and began his career with FC Barcelona. His extraordinary skills and humble demeanor have endeared him to fans worldwide. While Messi did not play for a Buenos Aires club, his impact on Argentine football is undeniable. His influence can be felt in the city's football culture, from the local clubs where young players dream of following in his footsteps, to the passionate discussions about football in cafes and bars across the city.

These personalities, each influential in their own right, have shaped the cultural fabric of Buenos Aires. Their stories and legacies are woven into the city's streets, its music, its art, and its people. As you explore Buenos Aires, you'll encounter their influence at every turn, adding depth and context to your understanding of this vibrant city.

II. Preparing for Your Trip

A. Best Time to Visit

Buenos Aires is a city that can be visited year-round, but the best time to visit largely depends on your preferences and interests. The city has a temperate climate with four distinct seasons, and there are different advantages and disadvantages to visiting during different times of the year.

Peak Season: The peak tourist season in Buenos Aires is from December to February, which is summertime in the Southern Hemisphere. During this time, the weather is warm and sunny, and there are plenty of outdoor festivals, concerts, and events taking place throughout the city. However, the peak season can also be the most crowded and expensive, with high hotel prices and long lines at popular attractions.

High Season: The high tourist season in Buenos Aires is from September to November and March to May. During these months, the weather is mild and pleasant, making it an ideal time for outdoor activities like strolling through the city's parks and gardens. There are also fewer crowds and lower hotel prices compared to the peak season.

Low Season: The low tourist season in Buenos Aires is from June to August, which is wintertime in the Southern Hemisphere. During this time, the weather can be cool and rainy, but there are still plenty of indoor activities like visiting museums and attending cultural events. The low season can also be a great time to visit if you're on a budget, as hotels and airfare tend to be cheaper.

Ultimately, the best time to visit Buenos Aires depends on your preferences and priorities. If you want to experience the city's vibrant nightlife and outdoor festivals, the peak season may be the best time to visit. However, if you're looking for a more relaxed and affordable trip, the high or low season may be a better choice.

It's also worth noting that Buenos Aires is a city with a rich cultural heritage and a variety of year-round events and attractions. Whether you visit during the peak, high, or low season, there is always something to see and do in this vibrant and exciting city.

The Weather in Buenos Aires

Buenos Aires has a temperate climate with four distinct seasons, each with its own unique weather patterns and conditions. Here is a monthly breakdown of what you can expect from the weather in Buenos Aires throughout the year:

January: January is the height of summer in Buenos Aires, with hot and humid weather and temperatures ranging from 25°C to 35°C (77°F to 95°F). It is also a month of occasional thunderstorms and rainfall.

February: February is still very hot and humid in Buenos Aires, with average temperatures of around 28°C to 32°C (82°F to 90°F). Rainfall and thunderstorms continue to be a possibility.

March: March is still warm in Buenos Aires, with temperatures ranging from 20°C to 27°C (68°F to 81°F). Rainfall and thunderstorms are less common in March, but still possible.

April: April marks the beginning of autumn in Buenos Aires, with mild and comfortable temperatures ranging from 15°C to 23°C (59°F to 73°F). Rainfall is less common in April.

May: May is a mild and comfortable month in Buenos Aires, with temperatures ranging from 12°C to 19°C (54°F to 66°F). It is a dry month with little rainfall.

June: June is the beginning of winter in Buenos Aires, with cool temperatures ranging from 9°C to 16°C (48°F to 61°F). It is a dry month with little rainfall.

July: July is the coldest month in Buenos Aires, with temperatures ranging from 8°C to 15°C (46°F to 59°F). It is a dry month with little rainfall.

August: August is still cool in Buenos Aires, with temperatures ranging from 10°C to 17°C (50°F to 63°F). It is a dry month with little rainfall.

September: September marks the beginning of spring in Buenos Aires, with temperatures ranging from 13°C to 21°C (55°F to 70°F). Rainfall increases in September.

October: October is a mild and pleasant month in Buenos Aires, with temperatures ranging from 15°C to 24°C (59°F to 75°F). Rainfall is common in October.

November: November is warm and often humid in Buenos Aires, with temperatures ranging from 18°C to 28°C (64°F to 82°F). Rainfall is common in November.

December: December marks the beginning of summer in Buenos Aires, with hot and humid weather and temperatures ranging from 23°C to 33°C (73°F to 91°F). Rainfall and thunderstorms are common in December.

Overall, Buenos Aires has a mild and comfortable climate for most of the year, with warm summers and cool winters. However, it is important to be prepared for occasional rainfall and thunderstorms, particularly in the summer months.

B. Visa and Entry Requirements

Before traveling to Buenos Aires, it is essential to familiarize yourself with the visa and entry requirements for Argentina. Visitors from many countries, including the United States, Canada, Australia, and the European Union, do not require a visa for stays of up to 90 days for tourism purposes. However, it is always a good idea to check the most up-to-date information with the Argentine consulate or embassy in your country.

All visitors must have a valid passport with at least six months of remaining validity from the date of entry. You may also be required to show proof of onward travel and sufficient funds to cover your stay.

C. Currency and Money Matters

The official currency of Argentina is the **Argentine Peso (ARS).** You can exchange your currency at banks, exchange bureaus, or hotels. ATMs are widely available in Buenos Aires and accept most major international credit and debit cards, although it's a good idea to check with your bank about any additional fees.

Credit cards are accepted in most hotels, restaurants, and shops, but it is always a good idea to carry some cash for smaller establishments or street vendors. It is also worth noting that some businesses offer a discount for cash payments due to high credit card fees in Argentina.

D. Health and Safety Tips

Buenos Aires is generally a safe city for tourists, but it is essential to take precautions to ensure a trouble-free trip.

- Be aware of your surroundings and keep an eye on your belongings, particularly in crowded areas or on public transportation.
- Avoid walking alone in unfamiliar areas, especially at night.
- Store valuables, such as passports, extra cash, and important documents, in a secure place like a hotel safe.
- Be cautious when using ATMs and shield your PIN when entering it.

In terms of health, tap water in Buenos Aires is safe to drink, but you may prefer bottled water if you are sensitive to changes in water quality. No specific vaccinations are required for Argentina, but it is a good idea to consult your doctor before your trip to ensure your routine vaccinations are up to date.

E. Packing Essentials

When packing for your trip to Buenos Aires, consider the following essentials:

1. Weather-appropriate clothing: Buenos Aires experiences four distinct seasons, so pack according to the time of year you plan to visit. Layers are always a good idea, as the weather can change throughout the day.

2. Comfortable walking shoes: The city is best explored on foot, so comfortable shoes are a must.

3. Electrical adapter and converter: Argentina uses Type I plugs and operates on a 220V power supply. Bring the appropriate adapters and converters to charge your electronic devices.

4. A small umbrella or rain jacket: Rain can be unpredictable in Buenos Aires, so it's a good idea to be prepared.

5. A Spanish phrasebook or translation app: While many people in Buenos Aires speak English, having some basic Spanish phrases at hand can be helpful in more local or off-the-beaten-path situations.

By being prepared with the necessary documents, packing the right items, and taking health and safety precautions, you will be well-equipped for a smooth and enjoyable trip to Buenos Aires.

F. Useful Information about Buenos Aires

Official Language: The Spanish Language is the official language.

Time Zone: GMT – 3 hours

Metric System: Kilograms, centimeters and Celsius

Weather: Warmest month is February and coldest month is July.

Buenos Aires, Argentina
Weather averages

Overview Graphs

Month	High / Low (°F)	Rain
January	84° / 69°	8 days
February	82° / 68°	7 days
March	78° / 65°	8 days
April	72° / 59°	7 days
May	65° / 53°	5 days
June	60° / 48°	5 days
July	59° / 47°	6 days
August	62° / 49°	6 days
September	65° / 52°	6 days
October	71° / 57°	8 days
November	76° / 62°	8 days
December	82° / 67°	8 days

Buenos Aires, Argentina
Weather averages

Overview Graphs

Month	High / Low (°C)	Rain
January	29° / 21°	8 days
February	28° / 20°	7 days
March	26° / 19°	8 days
April	22° / 15°	7 days
May	19° / 12°	5 days
June	16° / 9°	5 days
July	15° / 8°	6 days
August	17° / 10°	6 days
September	18° / 11°	6 days
October	22° / 14°	8 days
November	25° / 17°	8 days
December	28° / 19°	8 days

Electricity: Sockets and plugs in Buenos Aires are completely different than in US, so you will need an adapter. Argentina uses 220Volt and 50 KHz with Plug Type I, as below:

Currency: Argentina uses the Argentine peso (symbol: $), code ARS. Banknotes come in denominations of 100, 50, 20, 10, 5 and 2 pesos. Peso is subdivided into 100 centavos. Coins come in denominations of 2 and 1 pesos and 50, 25, 10 and 5 centavos.

Tipping: Tipping is generally not expected in Argentina. If you want to provide a tip, then give a 10% in restaurants, round up in the taxi, and 10% to your tour guide.

Cost of Living:

- Meal in an inexpensive restaurant: 7.5 USD
- Meal in a mid-range restaurant for two persons: 30 USD
- 0.33 liter of Water: 1 USD
- Local Transport (one-way ticket): 0.33 USD
- Cost of a bottle of Beer in a Bar: 2.22 USD
- Double room at an average hotel: 80 USD/night

Average Internet Speed: 4.7 Mbps (around 60% slower than in the US). The Wi-Fi coverage is moderate, and it is relatively easy to find free wifi at busy places.

Credit Cards: Visa and Mastercard are the most accepted credit cards. The small restaurants and shops may not accept credit cards. Sometimes you will be asked to show your passport when paying with a credit card. Some other times you may be asked to pay a small surcharge for paying with a credit card.

Dial Code: +54

Health Insurance: If you are coming from Europe bring your EHIC (European health insurance card). More info at http://ec.europa.eu/social/main.jsp?catId=1021&langId=en&intPageId=1728

Vaccinations: No vaccinations are requested to enter the country. You can check the status at https://www.iamat.org/country/austria/risk/routine-immunizations

Lost or Stolen Credit Card:

- American Express: +1 514 285 8165
- Diners Club: +1 514 877 1577
- Discover: +1 801 902 3100
- JCB: +81 3 5778 8379
- Mastercard: +1 636 722 7111
- Visa: +1 303 967 1096

Visa Requirements: It depends on the country of your whether you should get a Visa to enter Argentina. Please check https://www.visahq.com/ for more information.

Safety:

Like any big city, Buenos Aires has its share of safety concerns and scams to be aware of. Here are some tips to help you stay safe during your trip:

- Be cautious in crowded areas, such as public transport, markets, and tourist attractions, as pickpocketing can be common.
- Avoid walking alone at night in deserted areas, and always use well-lit streets. Stick to popular tourist areas and avoid walking through unfamiliar neighborhoods.
- Only use registered taxis or ride-sharing services, and be wary of unmarked taxis. Be sure to negotiate a price before getting into a taxi to avoid getting overcharged.
- Be cautious of people approaching you in the street to sell goods or services, especially those who seem overly persistent. These can be scams to distract you while their accomplices pick your pocket.

- Avoid giving money to beggars, as this can attract unwanted attention and potentially lead to theft.
- Be wary of scams involving money exchange, such as changing money on the street or using unofficial money exchange services. Always use official exchange offices or withdraw money from ATMs located in secure areas.
- Finally, be careful when using credit cards, and try to keep an eye on your card during transactions to avoid being overcharged.

By following these tips and remaining alert, you can help ensure a safe and enjoyable trip to Buenos Aires.

In case of an emergency while in Buenos Aires, it's important to know the local emergency numbers. The following are the most important numbers to keep on hand:

- Police: 911
- Ambulance: 107
- Fire Department: 100

It's always a good idea to keep a list of emergency contacts and important phone numbers on hand, in case of any unexpected situations. Additionally, if you're traveling with a mobile phone, consider adding these numbers to your contacts list for easy access.

If you're a foreign national traveling in Buenos Aires, it's also important to know the contact details for your country's embassy or consulate. In case of an emergency or if you need help with passport or visa issues, these embassies can provide assistance. Here are the contact details for some of the top embassies in Buenos Aires:

- United States Embassy: Av. Colombia 4300, C1425GMN CABA, Buenos Aires, Argentina; Tel: +54-11-5777-4533
- United Kingdom Embassy: Dr. Luis Agote 2412, C1425EOF CABA, Buenos Aires, Argentina; Tel: +54-11-4808-2200
- Canadian Embassy: Tagle 2828, C1425EEH CABA, Buenos Aires, Argentina; Tel: +54-11-4802-6369

- Australian Embassy: Villanueva 1400, C1426BMJ CABA, Buenos Aires, Argentina; Tel: +54-11-4779-3500
- New Zealand Embassy: Villanueva 1400, C1426BMJ CABA, Buenos Aires, Argentina; Tel: +54-11-4124-1800

Remember, it's always better to be prepared and have these important phone numbers and embassy details on hand, just in case you need them during your trip to Buenos Aires.

G. Top Tips for Traveling to Buenos Aires

#1: If you decide to **move around in a taxi**, try to take those who have a sign that reads "Radio Taxi," since they belong to a cab affiliate company and are not independent drivers. Taking taxis in Buenos Aires is very safe when compared to most South American cities, but still, it's a good idea to take this extra caution to avoid any kind of problem.

#2: **Avoid taking the metro between 7 AM to 10 AM and between 4 PM to 7 PM**. It gets really crowded to a point on which you may feel like you're in some kind of version of hell.

#3: If you arrive at Ezeiza (EZE) / Ministro Pistarini International Airport, **don't take the taxis right outside its doors**. You will find dozens of drivers offering to take you to the city, but they are not a good choice because they will find any possible way to charge you much more than what they say finally. Some of them aren't even real taxi drivers, but thieves are looking to steal your stuff. Hire any of the official transports that get you to the city (vans, buses, or official taxis). The airport is about 40 minutes away from the city's downtown, and the price of a regular service from the airport to any part of the city is approximate $15, while a taxi may be around $25.

#4: **Public transport is overall pretty safe and reliable** within the city. All buses work 24/7 and usually don't need to be waited at for more than a few minutes. Metro closes at 10:30 PM at night. All public transport is very cheap too when compared to Europe or USA standards.

#5: Try to learn some basic Spanish: Lots of *porteños* (a slang term for Buenos Aires citizens) don't speak fluent English, so it's always a good idea to learn a couple of basic words and questions in Spanish in case you need to use them.

#6: Try not to hang around downtown after midnight: Buenos Aires has very intense nightlife, but most of it goes on in other neighborhoods (mostly Palermo) and not at city center. If you hang around downtown after 1 AM you will probably not find a single soul in there.

#7: Avoid traveling to Buenos Aires in summer: The weather gets extremely hot during December, January and February. The combination of the heat and the humidity makes it really unpleasant to walk and go around the city. Plus, in January all *porteños* get away from the city, and many places are closed for the entire month. So do yourself a favor and go at any other time of the year. Buenos Aires is best enjoyed during fall and spring, but it's not a bad idea to go during the winter either since it doesn't get very cold.

H. The Best Tours and Activities to Pre-Book Before Going to Buenos Aires

Here, we have compiled a list of the most interesting and best-reviewed tours you can book before going to Buenos Aires. It includes activities such as Milonga night out, sightseeing tours of Buenos Aires, Tour to the River Plate and Boca Juniors Stadiums, Tigre Delta Boat trips and other. Click on the links to discover more about the prices, read the reviews of others and book anything that relates to your interests.

1. Highlights of Buenos Aires: Small Group 3-Hour Guided Tour (https://bit.ly/buenosaireshighlights):

This tour is perfect for those who want to get an overview of Buenos Aires' most iconic landmarks. In a small group setting, you'll explore the city's rich history, culture, and architecture, visiting places like the Plaza de Mayo, San Telmo, and La Boca. The tour is led by a knowledgeable guide who will provide insightful commentary throughout the journey.

2. Tigre Delta Boat trip from Buenos Aires
(https://bit.ly/buenosairestigre)

Escape the hustle and bustle of Buenos Aires with a serene boat trip to the Tigre Delta. This tour offers a unique perspective of the city's surroundings, as you navigate through the lush waterways and observe the charming houses on stilts. It's a refreshing break from the city and a chance to connect with nature.

3. Tigre Delta Premium Small-Group Tour from Buenos Aires
(https://bit.ly/buenosairestigre2):

This premium tour takes the Tigre Delta experience to the next level. In a small group, you'll explore the delta's natural beauty, visit the Paseo Victoria, and enjoy a traditional lunch at a riverside restaurant. The tour also includes a visit to the San Isidro neighborhood, known for its colonial architecture.

4. Buenos Aires: Piazzolla Tango Show with Dinner and Drinks
(https://bit.ly/buenosairestango1)

Immerse yourself in the vibrant culture of Buenos Aires with an evening of tango. This tour includes a delicious dinner, drinks, and a mesmerizing tango show at the Piazzolla Theatre. It's a perfect way to experience the passion and rhythm of Argentina's most famous dance.

5. Buenos Aires: Santa Susana Ranch Day Tour, BBQ & Shows
(https://bit.ly/buenosairessantasusana)

Experience the Argentine countryside with a day tour to Santa Susana Ranch. Here, you'll enjoy a traditional 'asado' (BBQ), watch a thrilling horse-riding show, and even have the chance to ride a horse or a 'sulky' (a type of horse-drawn carriage). It's a great way to experience Argentina's gaucho culture.

6. Colonia City Full Day Tour from Buenos Aires
(https://bit.ly/buenosairescolonia)

Take a day trip to the charming city of Colonia, Uruguay. This UNESCO World Heritage site is known for its cobblestone streets and colonial-era buildings. The tour includes a ferry ride across the Rio de la Plata, a guided tour of the city, and some free time to explore on your own.

7. Buenos Aires: Half-Day Sightseeing Tour (https://bit.ly/buenosaireshalfday)

If you're short on time, this half-day sightseeing tour is a great way to see Buenos Aires' main attractions. The tour covers key sites like the Obelisk, Plaza de Mayo, and the colorful neighborhood of La Boca. It's a quick but comprehensive introduction to the city.

8. El Viejo Almacen Tango Tickets and Dinner: Buenos Aires (https://bit.ly/42VcuN2)

Spend an unforgettable evening at El Viejo Almacen, one of Buenos Aires' oldest and most respected tango venues. The tour includes dinner, drinks, and a tango show that will leave you spellbound. It's a must-do for any visitor to Buenos Aires.

9. Full-Day at Santa Susana Ranch with BBQ, Drinks and Show (https://bit.ly/3peIQUU)

This full-day tour to Santa Susana Ranch offers a deep dive into Argentina's gaucho culture. You'll enjoy a traditional BBQ lunch, watch a folkloric show, and have the opportunity to go horseback riding or take a carriage ride. It's a fun and interactive way to learn about rural Argentine traditions.

10. Buenos Aires: 30-Minute City Tour by Helicopter (https://bit.ly/42Mdbb5)

For a truly unique perspective of Buenos Aires, take to the skies with a 30-minute helicopter tour. You'll soar over the city's sprawling landscape, taking in panoramic views of landmarks like the Obelisk, La Boca, and the River Plate Stadium. It's an exhilarating experience that offers unparalleled photo opportunities.

11. Buenos Aires: Skip-the-Line Colon Theater and Palaces Tour (https://bit.ly/46nk4D0)

Skip the line and dive into the world of music and architecture with a tour of the Colon Theater and Buenos Aires' palaces. The Colon Theater is one of the world's best opera houses, and this tour gives you a behind-the-scenes look at its stunning interiors. The tour also includes visits to the city's most opulent palaces, showcasing Buenos Aires' European influences.

12. Buenos Aires Airport Private Transfers to Downtown Hotels (https://bit.ly/3CDTLe5)

Start your Buenos Aires adventure with ease with a private transfer from the airport to your downtown hotel. This service ensures a hassle-free arrival, with a professional driver to navigate the city's busy streets. It's a convenient and comfortable way to begin your stay in Buenos Aires.

13. River Plate & Boca Juniors Stadiums Tour (https://bit.ly/3CBJDT5)

Football fans will love this tour of the River Plate and Boca Juniors stadiums. You'll get a behind-the-scenes look at these iconic stadiums, learn about the fierce rivalry between the two teams, and even have a chance to step onto the pitch. It's a must-do for any sports enthusiast.

14 Private Montevideo Tour + Lunch with Ferry from Buenos Aires (https://bit.ly/464RICN)

Take a day trip to Montevideo, the capital of Uruguay, with this private tour. The tour includes a ferry ride across the Rio de la Plata, a guided tour of Montevideo's highlights, and a delicious lunch. It's a great way to experience a different culture and see more of the region.

15. Buenos Aires Bike Tour: South or North Circuit (https://bit.ly/3NAsyPz)

Explore Buenos Aires on two wheels with a bike tour of the city's north or south circuit. This active tour is a fun way to see the city, with routes that cover key attractions like the Recoleta Cemetery and the colorful houses of La Boca. It's a great option for those who prefer a more active sightseeing experience.

16. Tango in Buenos Aires: 2-Hour Accompanied Milonga Outing (https://bit.ly/3XISGkz)

Experience the authentic tango culture of Buenos Aires with a 2-hour outing to a local 'milonga' (tango dance event). You'll be accompanied by a guide who will help you navigate the social codes of the milonga and even give you some dance tips. It's a unique and immersive way to experience the city's vibrant nightlife.

I. The bucket List for Buenos Aires

Buenos Aires is a city with a rich cultural heritage and a vibrant and cosmopolitan atmosphere. With so much to see and do, it can be challenging to decide how to make the most of your time in the city. Here are some top must-see things and must-do experiences to add to your bucket list for a three-day trip to Buenos Aires:

Tango Show and Dance Lesson: Tango is an essential part of Argentine culture and a must-see experience for visitors to Buenos Aires. Attend a tango show to experience the passion and energy of this iconic dance, or take a tango lesson to learn the basic steps and try your hand at this challenging and beautiful dance form.

Recoleta Cemetery: Recoleta Cemetery is a historic cemetery in Buenos Aires that is home to the graves of many famous and influential Argentinians, including Eva Perón. The cemetery is known for its ornate mausoleums and beautiful architecture, making it a fascinating destination for history and architecture lovers.

Visit La Boca: La Boca is a colorful and vibrant neighborhood in Buenos Aires, known for its brightly colored buildings and lively street performers. Visit the famous Caminito street to see tango performances, local artists, and street vendors selling handmade crafts and souvenirs.

San Telmo Market: The San Telmo Market is a popular destination for foodies and shoppers alike. This historic market is home to a wide variety of food stalls, antique shops, and local vendors selling everything from handmade crafts to vintage clothing.

Teatro Colón: Teatro Colón is one of the most beautiful and historic opera houses in the world, and a must-see destination for anyone interested in music or architecture. Take a guided tour to learn about the history of the theater and its stunning design, or attend a performance to experience the beauty of live opera or ballet.

Plaza de Mayo: Plaza de Mayo is a historic public square in the heart of Buenos Aires, and an important site for many of Argentina's most significant political and cultural events. Visit the square to see the iconic Casa Rosada (the presidential palace) and take a guided tour to learn about the history of this important public space.

Museums: Buenos Aires is home to a wide variety of museums and cultural institutions, including the Museum of Latin American Art of Buenos Aires (MALBA), the National Historical Museum, and the Museum of Immigration. These museums provide a deeper insight into the history and culture of Argentina and are must-visit destinations for anyone interested in learning more about the country.

Visit Palermo: Palermo is one of the trendiest neighborhoods in Buenos Aires, known for its hip restaurants, boutique shops, and lively nightlife. Visit the Botanical Garden, or explore the many street art murals and galleries in the neighborhood.

Boca Juniors Football Match: For sports fans, attending a Boca Juniors football match is a thrilling and unforgettable experience. Known for their passionate fans and legendary players, the Boca Juniors are one of the most famous and successful football teams in the world.

Try the Food: No trip to Buenos Aires would be complete without trying some of the city's famous cuisine. Sample traditional Argentine dishes like asado (barbecue), empanadas (meat-filled pastries), and dulce de leche (a sweet caramel-like spread).

These are just a few of the top must-see things and must-do experiences to add to your bucket list for a three-day trip to Buenos Aires. With so much to see and do in this vibrant and exciting city, there is no shortage of ways to make the most of your time and create unforgettable memories of your travels.

III. Transportation

A. Arriving in Buenos Aires

1. Airports

Buenos Aires is served by two main airports: **Ministro Pistarini International Airport** (Ezeiza, **EZE**) and **Aeroparque** Jorge Newbery (**AEP**).

Ministro Pistarini International Airport (Ezeiza):

Ezeiza is the primary international airport serving Buenos Aires and is located approximately 22 miles (35 km) south of the city center. Most international flights, including those from North America, Europe, and Asia, arrive and depart from Ezeiza. The airport has three terminals (A, B, and C) with various services, including currency exchange, ATMs, restaurants, and duty-free shops.

To get from Ezeiza to the city center, you have several options:

a. Taxi: Official taxis are available outside the arrivals area. The journey to the city center takes around 45 minutes to an hour, depending on traffic. You can either prepay for your taxi at an official booth inside the terminal or use a taxi-meter.

b. Private car or shuttle: Several companies offer private car or shuttle services, which can be booked in advance or upon arrival.

c. Public transportation: The public bus (line 8) connects the airport to the city center. Although it is the most economical option, it is also the slowest and may not be convenient if you have a lot of luggage.

Aeroparque Jorge Newbery (AEP):

Aeroparque is the domestic airport of Buenos Aires, located about 5 miles (8 km) from the city center. It handles regional flights to other Argentine cities and neighboring countries such as Uruguay, Brazil, and Chile. The airport offers various services, including ATMs, restaurants, and car rental agencies.

To get from Aeroparque to the city center, you can choose from the following options:

a. Taxi: Taxis are readily available outside the arrivals area. The journey to the city center takes about 15-20 minutes, depending on traffic.

b. Private car or shuttle: Like at Ezeiza, you can book a private car or shuttle service in advance or upon arrival.

c. Public transportation: Several bus lines connect the airport to different parts of the city. You can also take the local train from the nearby

Lisandro de la Torre station, which is a short taxi or bus ride away from the airport.

Upon arriving in Buenos Aires, it is essential to choose a transportation option that best suits your needs and preferences, ensuring a comfortable and hassle-free start to your trip.

How to Get from the Airport to the Center of Buenos Aires

Ezeiza (EZE) / Ministro Pistarini International Airport is located 30 km (18 miles) from the center of the city. It's crucial to be aware of the different possibilities for getting to the city center from the airport because there is no public transport making this ride.

There are basically two recommended ways of going from the International Airport to the heart of the city:

Get a Taxi: It costs between $20 and $25 to get to the center of the city. If you decide to go in a cab, it's important to get an official cab and not go with the independent drivers that are waiting right outside the airport. Inside the airport, you will find the official taxi companies' counters. Go there and ask for a taxi. Below you can see a picture of how the official taxi company counter looks like.

Get a Transfer Service: These are vans that take you to the city. They cost less than a taxi (around $15) and have a few predefined stops inside the city (Obelisk, Palermo, Recoleta, etc.). If one of those stops is near where you need to go, then this becomes a pretty good option. They usually depart every half an hour and take about 45 minutes to get to the Obelisk from the airport. Below you can see how one of these Transfer Services counters looks like. Just go there and ask for prices and times of departures.

If you want a private transfer, book it at Buenos Aires Airport Private Transfers to Downtown Hotels (https://bit.ly/3CDTLe5)

2. Bus Terminals

Buenos Aires has several bus terminals that connect the city to various destinations within Argentina and neighboring countries. The two main bus terminals in Buenos Aires are Retiro Bus Terminal and Terminal Dellepiane.

Retiro Bus Terminal:

Located adjacent to Retiro train station and close to the city center, Retiro Bus Terminal (Terminal de Ómnibus de Retiro) is the largest and busiest bus station in Buenos Aires. It serves long-distance buses to many domestic and international destinations, including popular tourist spots such as Mendoza, Bariloche, Iguazu Falls, and Montevideo (Uruguay). The terminal has three levels, with various facilities such as ticket offices, luggage storage, ATMs, currency exchange, restaurants, and shops.

To get to and from **Retiro Bus Terminal**, you can use the following transportation options:

a. Taxi: Taxis are available outside the terminal and can be a convenient option for reaching your accommodation.

b. Subte (subway): Retiro station on Line C is located a short walk from the bus terminal, connecting you to other parts of the city.

c. Public buses: Numerous bus lines serve the Retiro terminal, providing connections to different neighborhoods in Buenos Aires.

Terminal Dellepiane:

Opened in 2017, Terminal Dellepiane is a newer bus terminal in Buenos Aires, located approximately 4 miles (7 km) southwest of the city center. It mainly serves medium and short-distance routes within Argentina, including destinations in the provinces of Buenos Aires, Santa Fe, and Córdoba.

To get to and from Terminal Dellepiane, you can use the following transportation options:

a. Taxi: Taxis can be found outside the terminal, offering a convenient way to reach your destination.

b. Public buses: Several bus lines connect Terminal Dellepiane with different areas of the city.

When arriving in Buenos Aires by bus, it is crucial to plan your onward transportation to ensure a smooth and stress-free start to your visit.

B. Public Transportation

Buenos Aires has an extensive public transportation network, making it easy and affordable to navigate the city. The two primary modes of public transport are the Subte (subway) and colectivos (buses).

1. Subte (Subway)

The Subte, short for "Subterráneo," is Buenos Aires' underground metro system. With six lines (A, B, C, D, E, and H) covering over 36 miles (58 km) and serving 86 stations, the Subte is a quick and convenient way to travel around the city.

Fares: A single journey on the Subte costs ARS 30 (as of September 2021, subject to change). You can also purchase a rechargeable SUBE card, which allows you to travel on the Subte, colectivos, and trains at a discounted rate.

Operating Hours: The Subte runs from around 5:00 AM to 10:30 PM Monday through Saturday and from 8:00 AM to 10:30 PM on Sundays and public holidays. Trains operate every 3 to 10 minutes, depending on the time of day and the line.

Useful Tips:

- You can find a map of the Subte network on the official website (https://www.metrovias.com.ar/). You can also get the below map at https://subtebuenosaires.com.ar/mapa/

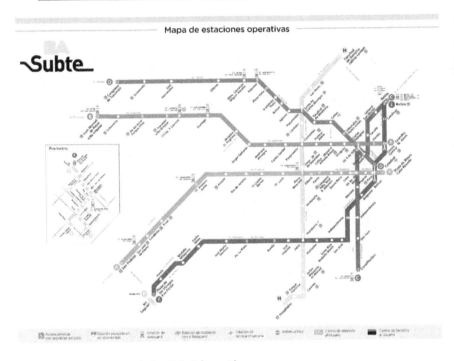

- **Google Maps** and the **BA Cómo Llego** app (https://apps.apple.com/us/app/ba-c%C3%B3mo-llego/id576489186) are useful tools for planning your journey on the Subte and other public transportation options in Buenos Aires. You can download all the Google Maps for Buenos Aires so as to have offline access. Here is some information on how to do it: https://blog.google/products/maps/google-maps-offline/

2. Colectivos (Buses)

Colectivos are Buenos Aires' extensive network of public buses, with over 140 lines connecting various neighborhoods throughout the city. They are a reliable and affordable mode of transportation, often operating 24 hours a day.

Fares: Colectivo fares are calculated based on the distance traveled, ranging from ARS 22 to ARS 33. You will need a **SUBE** card to pay for your colectivo rides.

Useful Tips:

- You can find route maps and timetables on the official website (https://www.buenosaires.gob.ar/subte/).

- Google Maps and the BA Cómo Llego app are helpful tools for planning your colectivo journeys.

- When boarding the colectivo, tell the driver your destination or the number of sections you will travel, and they will charge the appropriate fare to your SUBE card.

- Colectivos can get crowded during peak hours, so be prepared to stand and keep an eye on your belongings.

Using public transportation in Buenos Aires is not only budget-friendly but also an authentic way to experience the city like a local. Familiarize yourself with the routes, schedules, and fare systems to make the most of your time in this vibrant metropolis.

3. Taxis and Ride-Sharing Apps

Taxis and ride-sharing apps are another convenient option for getting around Buenos Aires, especially when public transportation is not available or suitable for your needs.

Taxis: Buenos Aires has a large fleet of taxis, which are easily recognizable by their black and yellow color scheme. Taxis can be hailed on the street, found at designated taxi stands, or ordered by phone. Fares are metered, with a base rate plus a charge per kilometer traveled. There may also be additional surcharges for waiting time, luggage, or nighttime travel.

Useful Tips:

- Only use official taxis with clearly visible taxi signs, working meters, and license information displayed.

- It's a good idea to have a rough estimate of the fare or route to your destination to avoid overcharging or being taken on unnecessary detours.

Ride-Sharing Apps: Ride-sharing services like **Uber, Cabify, and Beat** are available in Buenos Aires and can be a more convenient and comfortable alternative to traditional taxis. These apps allow you to request a ride, track your driver's location, and pay for the trip using your smartphone.

Useful Tips:

- Make sure you have a local SIM card or a reliable internet connection to use these apps.

- Ride-sharing services may sometimes face opposition from local taxi drivers, so it's best to be discreet when using them, particularly at busy locations like airports or bus terminals.

C. Renting a Car or Bicycle

Renting a car or bicycle can offer greater flexibility and independence when exploring Buenos Aires. Here are some considerations for each option:

Renting a Car:

Numerous car rental agencies, both international and local, operate in Buenos Aires. You can find rental offices at airports, in the city center, and in popular tourist areas.

Requirements: To rent a car, you must be at least 21 years old, have a valid driver's license from your home country, and possess an international driving permit (IDP). Most agencies also require a credit card for security deposits.

Useful Tips:

- Traffic in Buenos Aires can be hectic, and parking can be difficult and expensive in some areas. Consider renting a car only if you plan to explore destinations outside the city or if you are comfortable navigating urban traffic.

- Familiarize yourself with local driving rules and customs, such as the mandatory use of seatbelts, and be aware of the city's one-way streets and restricted traffic zones.

Renting a Bicycle: Buenos Aires has an extensive network of bike lanes, making cycling a convenient and eco-friendly option for getting around the city. Many bike rental shops offer a range of bicycles, from standard city bikes to electric and folding models.

Useful Tips:

- When renting a bicycle, make sure it is in good working condition and that you are provided with a helmet and lock for safety.

- Familiarize yourself with the city's bike lanes and recommended cycling routes, which can be found on maps and websites such as the official Buenos Aires tourism site (https://turismo.buenosaires.gob.ar/en/otros-establecimientos/bike-lanes).

- Always follow traffic rules and exercise caution when cycling in busy areas.

D. Navigating the City

Maps and Apps: To help you navigate Buenos Aires, consider using a combination of physical maps and digital tools. Physical maps can be found at tourist information centers and hotels, while digital tools like Google Maps and the BA Cómo Llego app offer real-time navigation, public transportation routes, and traffic updates.

Orientation: Buenos Aires is divided into 48 neighborhoods or "barrios," each with its own distinct character and attractions. The city's layout is generally a grid pattern, with Avenida 9 de Julio, one of the world's widest avenues, running through its center. Major streets, such as Avenida Corrientes and Avenida Santa Fe, can help you get your bearings as you explore the city.

Language: While many people in Buenos Aires speak English, especially in tourist areas, having some basic Spanish phrases and a translation app can be helpful when navigating the city and interacting with locals.

By familiarizing yourself with the various transportation options and equipping yourself with the right tools and knowledge, you can confidently navigate Buenos Aires and make the most of your visit to this vibrant and diverse city.

IV. Accommodations

A. Hotels

Buenos Aires offers a wide range of hotels to suit different budgets and preferences. From luxury hotels to boutique establishments and budget-friendly options, you can find the perfect accommodation to meet your needs.

Luxury Hotels: Notable luxury hotels in Buenos Aires include **Alvear Palace Hotel, Park Hyatt Buenos Aires, and Four Seasons Hotel Buenos Aires**.

Boutique Hotels: Boutique hotels in Buenos Aires combine personalized service with unique designs, often reflecting the city's rich history and culture. Some popular boutique hotels are **Home Hotel, Vitrum Hotel, and Palo Santo Hotel.**

Budget Hotels: For those looking for a more budget-friendly option, Buenos Aires has numerous affordable hotels that provide comfortable rooms and essential amenities without breaking the bank. Examples of budget hotels include **Ibis Buenos Aires, Hotel Babel, and Art Factory San Telmo.**

B. Hostels

Hostels in Buenos Aires cater to travelers seeking budget-friendly accommodations with a more social atmosphere. They often provide dormitory-style rooms with shared facilities, as well as private rooms for those seeking more privacy. Many hostels also offer communal spaces like lounges and kitchens, where guests can meet and interact with fellow travelers.

Party Hostels: Some hostels in Buenos Aires are known for their lively atmosphere and social events, making them a popular choice among younger travelers and those looking to make new friends. Examples of party hostels include **Milhouse Hostel, The Pink House, and America Del Sur Hostel.**

Chill and Cultural Hostels: If you prefer a more relaxed environment, there are hostels in Buenos Aires that focus on providing a cozy and cultural experience for their guests. These hostels often organize activities such as tango lessons, walking tours, or cooking classes. Notable chill and cultural hostels include **Art Factory Palermo, Circus Hostel & Hotel, and Sabatico Travelers Hostel.**

C. Boutique and Luxury Options

In addition to the boutique and luxury hotels mentioned earlier, Buenos Aires also offers a variety of unique and upscale accommodation options for travelers seeking a memorable stay.

Historic Estancias: For a truly authentic Argentine experience, consider staying at a historic estancia (ranch) in the outskirts of Buenos Aires. These properties often feature beautifully restored buildings, lush gardens, and various outdoor activities such as horseback riding and traditional Argentine barbecues (asados). Examples of historic estancias include **Estancia Villa Maria, Estancia La Bandada, and Estancia Candelaria del Monte.**

Luxury Apartments: Upscale serviced apartments offer the comforts of home with the amenities of a hotel. These apartments are ideal for those seeking more space, privacy, and the flexibility to cook their own meals. Some popular luxury apartment options in Buenos Aires include **Alvear Icon Residences, Poetry Building, and Vitrum Suites.**

V. Neighborhoods and Districts

A. Palermo

Palermo is the largest and one of the most popular neighborhoods in Buenos Aires. Known for its vibrant atmosphere, tree-lined streets, and fashionable boutiques, Palermo is divided into several sub-districts, each with its unique charm.

Palermo Soho:

This trendy area is famous for its bohemian vibes, with a plethora of designer shops, art galleries, bars, and cafes. The cobblestone streets of Palermo Soho come alive at night, making it a popular nightlife destination.

Palermo Hollywood:

Named after the concentration of film and television production companies, Palermo Hollywood boasts numerous bars, clubs, and restaurants, offering an eclectic mix of cuisine and entertainment options.

Palermo Chico and Palermo Parks:

These upscale residential areas are characterized by their lush parks, embassies, and museums, such as the MALBA (Museum of Latin American Art of Buenos Aires) and the Evita Museum.

B. Recoleta

Recoleta is one of Buenos Aires' most elegant and sophisticated neighborhoods, known for its French-inspired architecture, upscale boutiques, and stylish cafes. Some of the main attractions in Recoleta include:

Recoleta Cemetery: This historic cemetery is the final resting place of many famous Argentine figures, including Eva Perón (Evita). Its ornate mausoleums and intricate sculptures make it a must-visit site.

Floralis Genérica: This impressive 66-foot (20-meter) tall steel flower sculpture opens and closes its petals with the sun's movement, symbolizing hope and rebirth.

Museo Nacional de Bellas Artes: The National Museum of Fine Arts houses an extensive collection of Argentine and international art, including works by renowned artists such as Monet, Van Gogh, and Picasso

C. San Telmo

San Telmo is one of the oldest neighborhoods in Buenos Aires, characterized by its colonial buildings, narrow streets, and rich history. This bohemian district offers visitors a glimpse into the city's past and a vibrant cultural scene.

San Telmo Market: This historic market, dating back to 1897, is a must-visit for its antique stalls, food vendors, and lively atmosphere.

Plaza Dorrego: The heart of San Telmo, Plaza Dorrego, is a bustling square surrounded by bars, cafes, and tango clubs. On Sundays, the square hosts the famous Feria de San Telmo, an antique and flea market where you can find unique souvenirs.

Tango Shows: San Telmo is known for its intimate tango clubs, or "milongas," where you can watch passionate performances or even take a tango lesson.

D. Puerto Madero

Puerto Madero is Buenos Aires' newest and most luxurious neighborhood, located along the Río de la Plata waterfront. Once a derelict port area, it has been transformed into a sleek and modern district with upscale restaurants, hotels, and residential towers.

Puente de la Mujer: This iconic pedestrian bridge, designed by Spanish architect Santiago Calatrava, symbolizes the unity of the city's past and present and serves as a popular photo spot.

Reserva Ecológica Costanera Sur: This expansive nature reserve is a green oasis within the city, offering walking and biking trails, birdwatching opportunities, and stunning views of the skyline.

Fortabat Art Collection: Housed in a striking modern building, this private museum showcases a diverse range of Argentine and international artwork from renowned artists such as Salvador Dalí and Andy Warhol.

E. Retiro

Retiro is a bustling central neighborhood known for its transportation hubs, shopping centers, and historic landmarks.

Plaza San Martín: This picturesque square, surrounded by elegant French-style buildings, serves as a peaceful retreat in the heart of the city.

Galerías Pacífico: This opulent shopping center, housed in a beautifully restored historic building, features a stunning frescoed dome and a wide selection of high-end shops and boutiques.

Torre Monumental: Formerly known as the Torre de los Ingleses, this clock tower commemorates the centenary of Argentine independence and offers panoramic views of the city from its observation deck.

F. Belgrano

Belgrano is a large, leafy neighborhood known for its diverse architecture, green spaces, and vibrant cultural scene.

Barrio Chino: Belgrano's bustling Chinatown offers a colorful array of shops, restaurants, and markets, making it an ideal destination for food lovers and souvenir hunters.

Plaza Barrancas de Belgrano: This charming park, featuring sloping terraces and a picturesque gazebo, is a popular spot for relaxation and recreation.

Museo de Arte Español Enrique Larreta: This museum, housed in a former residence, showcases an impressive collection of Spanish art and a beautiful Andalusian-style garden.

G. Almagro and Boedo

Almagro and Boedo are traditional working-class neighborhoods with strong cultural roots, known for their tango clubs, historic cafes, and lively community atmosphere.

Café Margot: This historic café, founded in 1904, retains its old-world charm and serves as a popular gathering spot for locals and visitors alike.

Tango Clubs: Almagro and Boedo are home to several authentic tango venues, such as La Catedral Club and El Cocomarola, where you can experience the passion and intensity of this iconic Argentine dance.

Parque Centenario: This spacious park offers a variety of recreational facilities, including a lake, an amphitheater, and the Bernardino Rivadavia Natural Sciences Museum.

Exploring these diverse neighborhoods will provide you with a well-rounded experience of Buenos Aires, allowing you to appreciate the city's unique character and rich cultural heritage.

VI. Dining and Nightlife

Buenos Aires is a city that loves to eat, drink, and celebrate. The dining and nightlife scene is diverse, vibrant, and offers something for everyone. From traditional Argentine cuisine to international fare, from cozy cafés to lively nightclubs, the city has it all. Discover the rich flavors and exciting experiences that await you in Buenos Aires.

A. Traditional Argentine Cuisine

Argentina is famous for its beef, and Buenos Aires is the perfect place to indulge in some of the world's finest steaks. However, traditional Argentine cuisine goes beyond just meat, with delicious regional dishes and flavors waiting to be discovered.

1. **Parrillas:**

Parrillas, or steakhouses, are an essential part of Argentine dining culture. These establishments serve up succulent cuts of beef, such as bife de chorizo, ojo de bife, and entraña, grilled to perfection over wood or charcoal fires. Some of the most famous parrillas in Buenos Aires include **La Cabrera, Don Julio, and El Mirasol.**

2. Empanadas:

These savory pastries, filled with various ingredients such as beef, chicken, cheese, or vegetables, are a popular snack or appetizer in Argentina. You can find empanadas at bakeries, street vendors, and dedicated empanada shops like La Continental, El Sanjuanino, and 1810 Cocina Regional.

3. **Milanesa:**

This breaded and fried meat dish, similar to a schnitzel, is another Argentine favorite. Typically made with beef or chicken, milanesas can be found at many restaurants and casual eateries throughout Buenos Aires.

4. **Pizza and Fugazzetta:**

With a significant Italian influence, Buenos Aires has developed its unique pizza style, characterized by a thick, doughy crust and generous toppings. Fugazzetta, a local variation of the classic pizza, features a double crust filled with cheese and topped with caramelized onions. Visit pizzerias such as El Cuartito, Güerrin, or Banchero to try these mouthwatering creations.

5. Asado:

The Argentine barbecue, or asado, is a social event where friends and family gather to share an array of grilled meats, sausages, and vegetables. While asados are typically held in private homes, some restaurants, like La Estancia or El Pobre Luis, offer an authentic asado experience.

6. Dulce de Leche:

Dulce de leche is a sweet and creamy caramel-like spread that is a staple of Argentine cuisine. It is often used as a filling for pastries, cakes, and other desserts.

7. **Choripán**:

Choripán is a traditional Argentine sandwich made with grilled chorizo sausage and bread. It is often served with chimichurri sauce, a flavorful blend of herbs, spices, and vinegar.

8. **Provoleta:**

Provoleta is a grilled provolone cheese that is a popular appetizer or side dish in Buenos Aires. It is typically served with bread and chimichurri sauce.

9. Matambre:

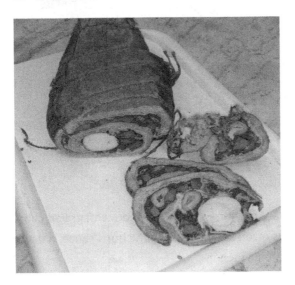

Matambre is a rolled and stuffed flank steak that is a popular dish in Argentina. It is often filled with vegetables, cheese, and other ingredients, then grilled or baked to perfection.

10. Locro:

Locro is a hearty stew that is made with corn, beans, meat, and other ingredients. It is a popular dish during the winter months and is often served with bread or empanadas.

11. Alfajores:

Alfajores are a sweet and indulgent dessert that consist of two soft cookies filled with dulce de leche and coated with powdered sugar or chocolate. They are a popular treat in Buenos Aires and can be found at many local bakeries and cafes.

12. **Fernet con Coca:** Fernet con Coca is a popular alcoholic drink in Argentina that consists of fernet, a bitter herbal liqueur, mixed with

Coca-Cola. It is often served as a digestif after a meal or as a social drink at bars and restaurants.

13. **Wine and Mate:** No Argentine meal is complete without a glass of **Malbec**, the country's most famous red wine. For a more casual beverage, try mate, a traditional herbal infusion shared among friends and family.

B. Cafés and Coffee Shops

Buenos Aires has a rich café culture, with traditional coffee shops known as "cafés notables" that have played a significant role in the city's history, as well as modern specialty coffee shops that cater to coffee enthusiasts. Here are a few noteworthy options:

1. **Café Tortoni** (www.cafetortoni.com.ar): One of the city's oldest and most famous cafés, Café Tortoni is a must-visit for its historic atmosphere, tango shows, and classic Argentine pastries. Prices range from ARS 150 to ARS 500 for coffee and snacks.

2. **Las Violetas** (www.lasvioletas.com): This elegant café, founded in 1884, is known for its beautiful stained-glass windows, lavish interior, and delicious afternoon tea service. Prices range from ARS 250 to ARS 800 for coffee, pastries, and light meals.

3. **LAB Tostadores de Café** (www.labcafe.com.ar): A modern specialty coffee shop in Palermo, LAB offers a range of expertly brewed single-origin coffees and a selection of light bites. Prices range from ARS 150 to ARS 450 for coffee and snacks.

4. **All Saints Café** (www.allsaintscafe.com.ar): With several locations across the city, All Saints Café is a popular spot for locals and visitors alike, serving high-quality coffee, pastries, and sandwiches. Prices range from ARS 150 to ARS 500 for coffee and light meals.

C. Steakhouses and Parrillas

As mentioned earlier, steakhouses and parrillas are an integral part of Buenos Aires' dining scene. Here are a few must-visit options:

1. **La Cabrera** (www.parrillalacabrera.com.ar): Located in Palermo, La Cabrera is one of the city's most renowned parrillas, known for its perfectly grilled steaks, generous portions, and attentive service. Prices range from ARS 800 to ARS 2,500 for main dishes.

2. **Don Julio** (www.parrilladonjulio.com.ar): Another popular steakhouse in Palermo, Don Julio offers a warm atmosphere, excellent cuts of beef, and an extensive wine list. Prices range from ARS 800 to ARS 2,500 for main dishes.

3. **El Mirasol** (www.elmirasol.com.ar): With several locations in Buenos Aires, El Mirasol is a classic parrilla that has been serving up delicious Argentine steaks for decades. Prices range from ARS 700 to ARS 2,200 for main dishes.

4. **La Brigada** (www.labrigada.com.ar): Located in San Telmo, La Brigada is a traditional parrilla with a cozy, rustic atmosphere, serving tender steaks and a variety of Argentine dishes. Prices range from ARS 700 to ARS 2,000 for main dishes.

D. Vegetarian and Vegan Options

Buenos Aires has embraced the growing trend of vegetarian and vegan cuisine, with an increasing number of restaurants catering to plant-based diets. Here are a few recommendations:

1. **Buenos Aires Verde** (www.bsasverde.com): With locations in Palermo and Belgrano, Buenos Aires Verde offers a creative menu of vegetarian and vegan dishes, including salads, wraps, and raw food options. Prices range from ARS 400 to ARS 1,200 for main dishes.

2. **Bio Solo Organico** (www.bio-restaurant.com.ar): Located in Palermo, this organic restaurant serves vegetarian and vegan cuisine made

with locally-sourced ingredients, along with fresh juices and smoothies. Prices range from ARS 300 to ARS 1,000 for main dishes.

3. **VITA** (www.vitarestaurant.com.ar): A modern vegan eatery in the city center, VITA offers a range of plant-based dishes, from burgers to sushi, as well as a selection of natural wines. Prices range from ARS 350 to ARS 900 for main dishes.

E. Wine and Cocktail Bars

Buenos Aires has a thriving wine and cocktail scene, with a diverse range of bars catering to all tastes. Here are a few options to consider:

1. **Florería Atlántico** (www.floreriaatlantico.com.ar): A hidden gem in Retiro, Florería Atlántico is a speakeasy-style cocktail bar located beneath a flower shop, offering creative cocktails and a curated wine list. Prices range from ARS 450 to ARS 1,000 for drinks.

2. **Gran Bar Danzón** (www.granbardanzon.com.ar): This sophisticated wine and cocktail bar in Recoleta boasts an extensive wine list, innovative cocktails, and a lively atmosphere. Prices range from ARS 400 to ARS 1,200 for drinks.

3. **Pain et Vin** (www.pain-et-vin.com): A cozy wine bar and bakery in Palermo, Pain et Vin offers a selection of Argentine wines by the glass, paired with artisanal bread and charcuterie. Prices range from ARS 300 to ARS 800 for wine and snacks.

F. The Top Wines to Try

Argentina is renowned for its wine production, and Buenos Aires is a great place to sample some of the country's finest wines. Here are the top 10 wines to try in Buenos Aires:

- **Malbec:** Malbec is Argentina's signature red wine, and it is widely regarded as one of the best in the world. This full-bodied wine is known for its dark fruit flavors, smooth tannins, and hints of chocolate and coffee.

- **Cabernet Sauvignon:** Cabernet Sauvignon is a rich and complex red wine that is also popular in Argentina. It is characterized by its deep red color, intense aromas of black currant and cedar, and firm tannins.
- **Torrontés:** Torrontés is a white wine that is unique to Argentina. It is known for its floral and citrus aromas, crisp acidity, and light body.
- **Bonarda:** Bonarda is another red wine that is becoming increasingly popular in Argentina. It is characterized by its dark fruit flavors, soft tannins, and smooth finish.
- **Syrah:** Syrah, also known as Shiraz, is a full-bodied red wine that is grown in many wine regions around the world, including Argentina. It is known for its spicy, peppery flavors, dark fruit aromas, and tannic structure.
- **Chardonnay:** Chardonnay is a popular white wine that is grown in many different wine regions, including Argentina. It is known for its buttery and oaky flavors, as well as its crisp acidity.
- **Pinot Noir:** Pinot Noir is a light-bodied red wine that is known for its delicate flavors of red fruit and earthy notes. It is a difficult grape to grow, but the cooler regions of Argentina produce some excellent Pinot Noir wines.
- **Merlot:** Merlot is a medium-bodied red wine that is known for its smooth tannins and flavors of dark fruit, chocolate, and tobacco. It is often blended with other grapes, such as Malbec or Cabernet Sauvignon.
- **Sauvignon Blanc:** Sauvignon Blanc is a popular white wine that is known for its crisp acidity and flavors of green apple, grapefruit, and grass. It is often grown in cooler regions of Argentina, such as the Uco Valley.
- **Red blends:** Many Argentine winemakers produce red blends that combine several different grape varieties. These blends can be complex and flavorful, with different grapes contributing their unique characteristics to the final product.

These are just a few of the many wines that you can try in Buenos Aires, which is home to many excellent wineries and wine bars. Whether you're a seasoned wine aficionado or simply looking to try something new, there is sure to be a wine in Buenos Aires that will satisfy your taste buds and give you a deeper appreciation for the country's rich wine culture.

G. Nightclubs and Live Music Venues

Buenos Aires is famous for its vibrant nightlife, with numerous nightclubs and live music venues catering to a variety of musical tastes. Here are a few options:

Niceto Club (www.nicetoclub.com): Located in Palermo, Niceto Club is one of the city's most popular nightclubs, hosting a range of live music and DJ events, including the famous Club 69 party on Thursdays. Prices range from ARS 300 to ARS 1,000 for entry and drinks.

La Trastienda (www.latrastienda.com): A renowned live music venue in San Telmo, La Trastienda hosts both local and international acts across various genres, from rock to tango. Prices vary depending on the event, with tickets typically ranging from ARS 400 to ARS 2,000.

Makena (www.makenacantinaclub.com): This lively nightclub and live music venue in Palermo features a mix of genres, from jazz and funk to electronic music, providing an eclectic experience for music lovers. Prices range from ARS 200 to ARS 700 for entry and drinks.

H. Our favorite Dining Places in Buenos Aires

Argentina has one of the most interesting gastronomy scenarios of the world, mainly thanks to the fabulous worldwide recognized meat.

We strongly recommend going to a *parrilla* and taste an amazing *asado* at least once, if not more. Another interesting Argentinian food you should definitely try is empanadas. Finally, you may also want to try some pizza in Buenos Aires, which is mainly famous due to the enormous amount of cheese they put into them.

Here are some of our favorite dining places in Buenos Aires:

- **La Cabrera** *(5099 José Antonio Cabrera Street, Palermo,* *http://lacabrera.com.ar/en/)*:

The most famous *parrilla* in the whole city. It can be a little pricey, and you will also find lots of tourists in here, but it's all worth it because you this is probably the best meat you will ever eat in your life. You should try to make a reservation in advance because it gets really crowded. It has a happy hour between 6:30 PM and 8 PM, on which you have a 40% discount on everything; the only downside of this is that they kick you out at 8 o'clock with no exception.

La Cabrera is a world-renowned steakhouse located in the upscale Palermo neighborhood of Buenos Aires. It has consistently been ranked as one of the best restaurants in the city, and it has become a must-visit destination for foodies and steak lovers from around the world.

The restaurant is known for its high-quality beef, which is sourced from local farms and carefully aged to perfection. The steaks are grilled over an open flame, giving them a delicious smoky flavor and a crispy outer crust. The menu also includes a variety of other meat dishes, including pork, chicken, and lamb, as well as seafood and vegetarian options.

In addition to its mouthwatering cuisine, La Cabrera is known for its warm and inviting atmosphere. The restaurant is housed in a charming brick building with a rustic interior, complete with exposed brick walls, wooden tables, and vintage decor. There is also an outdoor patio where diners can enjoy their meals in the open air.

Despite its popularity, La Cabrera manages to maintain a friendly and attentive staff, who are always willing to offer recommendations and explain the different cuts of meat on the menu. The portions are generous, so it's a good idea to bring a few friends and share a few dishes.

Pizzeria Guerrin (*1368 Corrientes Avenue, Downtown,* *http://www.pizzeriaguerrin.com*): Right next to all the famous Corrientes Avenue there is this mythic place with all its history. Make sure you like cheese because they put a lot of it to their pizzas.

If you're in the mood for some delicious pizza, head to Pizzeria Guerrin in Buenos Aires. This unassuming pizzeria has been serving up some of the best pies in the city for over 80 years.

Located in the heart of the city center, Pizzeria Guerrin has a simple and casual atmosphere that is perfect for a quick meal or a late-night snack. The menu is focused on pizza, and they offer a wide variety of toppings to choose from. Some of the most popular pies include the mozzarella, the ham and cheese, and the famous fugazzeta, which is a pizza topped with caramelized onions and cheese.

The pizza at Pizzeria Guerrin is cooked in a brick oven, which gives it a crispy and slightly charred crust. The toppings are fresh and flavorful, and the portions are generous. You can order your pizza by the slice or by the whole pie, and they also offer delivery for those who want to enjoy their pizza in the comfort of their own home.

Despite its popularity, Pizzeria Guerrin maintains a down-to-earth and friendly vibe. The staff are welcoming and always happy to help you choose the perfect pizza. The prices are also very reasonable, making it a great option for budget-conscious travelers.

Overall, Pizzeria Guerrin is a must-visit destination for pizza lovers in Buenos Aires. Whether you're looking for a quick lunch, a late-night snack, or a delicious dinner, this pizzeria has something to offer everyone. So grab a slice and enjoy the taste of authentic Argentine pizza at Pizzeria Guerrin.

La Casita de Tucumán (*1507 Ecuador Street, Recoleta,* *https://www.facebook.com/lacasitadetucuman/*): Some of the best empanadas you can have in Buenos Aires in this little cozy place located in the neighborhood of Recoleta.

La Casita de Tucumán is a small and unpretentious restaurant located in the San Telmo neighborhood of Buenos Aires. The restaurant is named after the city of Tucumán, which is known for its traditional Argentine dishes and ingredients.

The menu at La Casita de Tucumán focuses on authentic Argentine cuisine, with a particular emphasis on the dishes of the northern region of the country. Some of the most popular dishes include empanadas, humita (a savory corn pudding), locro (a hearty stew made with corn, beans, and meat), and tamales (a type of steamed corn dumpling).

The food at La Casita de Tucumán is simple, rustic, and delicious. The portions are generous, and the prices are very reasonable, making it a popular spot among locals and tourists alike. The restaurant has a casual and laid-back atmosphere, with wooden tables and chairs, colorful decorations, and a friendly staff.

One of the highlights of La Casita de Tucumán is its **empanadas,** which are made fresh to order and come in a variety of flavors, including beef, chicken, ham and cheese, and vegetarian options. They are crispy on the outside and filled with flavorful ingredients on the inside, making them a perfect snack or appetizer.

Overall, La Casita de Tucumán is a great spot for those looking to try authentic Argentine cuisine in a cozy and welcoming environment. The food is delicious, the prices are reasonable, and the atmosphere is unpretentious and laid-back. If you're in the San Telmo neighborhood, be sure to stop by La Casita de Tucumán for a taste of traditional Argentine flavors.

El Tejano (*4416 Honduras Street, Palermo,* *https://ahumadoras.com/eltejanoba/*): If you feel like trying something different than typical Argentinian food, you may want to check out this Texan place. Ribs and chicken wings at this place are without a doubt the best you will find in the entire city. The place is really tiny, so reservation beforehand is needed.

El Tejano is a lively and vibrant Tex-Mex restaurant located in the Palermo neighborhood of Buenos Aires. The restaurant offers a fun and casual atmosphere, perfect for a night out with friends or a family dinner.

The menu at El Tejano is inspired by the flavors of the American Southwest, with a focus on Tex-Mex cuisine. Some of the most popular dishes include tacos, fajitas, quesadillas, and burritos, all made with fresh ingredients and bold flavors. The restaurant also offers a selection of signature cocktails and beers to complement your meal.

The decor of El Tejano is rustic and colorful, with wooden tables and chairs, brightly colored walls, and an outdoor patio area. The restaurant often has live music or other entertainment, making it a popular spot for locals and tourists alike.

One of the highlights of El Tejano is its delicious margaritas, which are made with fresh lime juice and high-quality tequila. They come in a variety of flavors, including classic, mango, and strawberry, and are the perfect complement to a spicy Tex-Mex meal.

Overall, El Tejano is a fun and lively spot for those looking to enjoy Tex-Mex cuisine in Buenos Aires. The food is delicious, the drinks are refreshing, and the atmosphere is lively and welcoming. If you're in the Palermo neighborhood and in the mood for some Tex-Mex cuisine, be sure to stop by El Tejano for a taste of the American Southwest.

I. Where to Find the Best Empanadas in Buenos Aires

If you're in Buenos Aires and feel like eating **empanadas**, you will find every 100 meters. Even though most of them are usually pretty good, here we give you a list of the best among the best places for you to try this delicious Argentinian famous food.

#1: El Sanjuanino – Sánchez de Bustamante 1788, http://www.elsanjuanino.com.ar/

Typical place on which you'll find a public radio playing in the background and mostly old every-day customers at the tables. We recommend the ones of spicy meat, ham and cheese and blue cheese, but all of them are good.

#2: La Americana – Avenida Callao 83, https://www.monroeamericana.com.ar/

Opened in 1935, this place considers itself as "the Queen of Empanadas" (a statement you can even read on its walls). The type of empanadas that they offer here is *salteñas*, which means they are made in the style of **Salta**, a northern province of Argentina.

#3: La Fachada – Aráoz 1283, http://www.lafachada.com.ar/

You can eat on traditional tables or in a small living room with little tables. They have a great variety of different tastes.

#4 La Mezzetta – Álvarez Thomas 1311, https://www.facebook.com/pizzeria.lamezzetta

These empanadas come of an enormous size. You should not order more than 2 or 3 per person.

#5: La Morada – Hipólito Yrigoyen 778, http://www.lamorada.com.ar/

Apart from the amazing empanadas, a visit to this place is also worth it because of the walls decoration: it's like a retro pop collection. You'll find everything from 40's magazines to little toys from that era.

VII. Attractions and Sightseeing

A. Historical Sites and Monuments

Buenos Aires is rich in history, and exploring its many historical sites and monuments is a must for visitors. Here are a few noteworthy attractions:

Casa Rosada (www.casarosada.gob.ar):

The iconic pink presidential palace, located in the Plaza de Mayo, is an important symbol of Argentine history and politics. Free guided tours are available on weekends and public holidays, but reservations are required in advance.

El Obelisco:

This towering monument, located at the intersection of Avenida Corrientes and Avenida 9 de Julio, commemorates the city's founding and serves as a symbol of Buenos Aires. There is no admission fee to visit the monument.

Teatro Colón (www.teatrocolon.org.ar):

One of the world's most famous opera houses, Teatro Colón is an architectural masterpiece with a rich history. Guided tours are available daily, with prices ranging from ARS 800 to ARS 1,500 for adults, depending on the tour type.

B. Museums and Art Galleries

Buenos Aires boasts a diverse range of museums and art galleries, showcasing the city's artistic and cultural heritage. Here are a few recommendations:

1. **MALBA** (www.malba.org.ar): The Latin American Art Museum of Buenos Aires features a vast collection of modern and contemporary Latin American art. Admission costs ARS 500 for adults, with free entry on Wednesdays.

2. **Museo Nacional de Bellas Artes** (www.bellasartes.gob.ar): This museum houses an extensive collection of Argentine and

international artwork, including pieces by renowned artists such as Monet, Van Gogh, and Rembrandt. Admission is free.

3. **Museo de Arte Contemporáneo de Buenos Aires** (www.macba.com.ar): Located in San Telmo, this museum focuses on contemporary art from both local and international artists. Admission costs ARS 250 for adults, with free entry on Wednesdays.

4. **Usina del Arte** (www.usinadelarte.org): Housed in a beautifully restored former power plant in La Boca, the Usina del Arte hosts various art exhibitions, music performances, and cultural events. Most exhibitions and events are free, but some may require tickets.

C. Parks and Gardens

Buenos Aires is home to numerous parks and gardens, providing peaceful green spaces to relax and unwind amidst the bustling city. Here are a few notable options:

1. **Jardín Botánico Carlos Thays:** Located in Palermo, this beautiful botanical garden is home to over 5,000 plant species, sculptures, and historical buildings. Admission is free.

2. **Parque Tres de Febrero**: Also known as Bosques de Palermo, this expansive park features walking paths, lakes, rose gardens, and recreational areas. It's an ideal spot for picnics, jogging, or cycling. Admission is free.

3. **Reserva Ecológica Costanera Sur:** This ecological reserve along the Río de la Plata offers a unique opportunity to experience nature within the city. With walking trails, birdwatching opportunities, and beautiful views, the reserve is a tranquil escape from urban life. Admission is free.

D. Tango Shows and Dance Lessons

No visit to Buenos Aires would be complete without experiencing the passion and artistry of Argentine tango. Here are a few options to enjoy tango shows and take dance lessons:

1. Esquina Carlos Gardel (www.esquinacarlosgardel.com.ar): This elegant tango dinner show in Abasto pays homage to legendary tango singer Carlos Gardel, featuring a live orchestra and world-class dancers. Prices range from ARS 6,000 to ARS 10,000 for dinner and show packages.

2. La Ventana (www.la-ventana.com.ar): Located in San Telmo, La Ventana offers an intimate tango dinner show, showcasing traditional Argentine music and dance. Prices range from ARS 5,500 to ARS 9,000 for dinner and show packages.

3. DNI Tango (www.dni-tango.com/en): This tango school in Palermo offers group and private tango lessons for all skill levels, taught by experienced instructors. Prices range from ARS 1,000 to ARS 3,000 per lesson, depending on the class type and duration.

4. La Viruta (www.lavirutatango.com): A popular tango club in Palermo, La Viruta offers group tango lessons followed by a milonga (tango dance party) where you can practice your new moves. Prices range from ARS 400 to ARS 1,000 for lessons and entry to the milonga.

E. Sports Events and Stadiums

Buenos Aires is a city passionate about sports, with football (soccer) being the most popular. Attending a sports event or visiting a stadium can provide a unique and exciting glimpse into the city's vibrant sports culture. Here are a few options to consider:

1. La Bombonera (www.bocajuniors.com.ar): The iconic home stadium of Boca Juniors, one of Argentina's most successful football clubs, is located in the La Boca neighborhood. The atmosphere during a match is electrifying, and tickets can be purchased through the official club

website or authorized resellers. Prices range from ARS 1,000 to ARS 4,000, depending on seat location and match importance.

2. Estadio Monumental (www.cariverplate.com.ar): Home to River Plate, another major Argentine football club, the Estadio Monumental is located in the Belgrano neighborhood. Attending a match here is a thrilling experience, and tickets can be purchased through the official club website or authorized resellers. Prices range from ARS 1,000 to ARS 4,000, depending on seat location and match importance.

3. Estadio José Amalfitani (www.velezsarsfield.com.ar): Home to the Vélez Sarsfield football club, this stadium is located in the Liniers neighborhood. Tickets can be purchased through the official club website or authorized resellers, with prices typically ranging from ARS 800 to ARS 3,000.

4. Luna Park Stadium (www.lunapark.com.ar): This indoor arena, located in the San Nicolás neighborhood, hosts a variety of sporting events, including boxing, basketball, and tennis, as well as concerts and other entertainment events. Ticket prices vary depending on the event and seating preferences.

5. Buenos Aires Lawn Tennis Club (www.baltc.com.ar): This prestigious tennis club in Palermo hosts the Argentina Open, an annual ATP World Tour event, usually held in February. Ticket prices for the tournament vary, with daily passes typically ranging from ARS 1,500 to ARS 5,000, depending on the stage of the competition and seat location.

F. Day Trips and Excursions

Buenos Aires' location offers a variety of exciting day trips and excursions for those looking to explore beyond the city limits. Here are a few popular options:

1. **Tigre and Delta del Paraná** (www.tigre.gov.ar): Just a short train ride from Buenos Aires, the town of Tigre and the surrounding Paraná Delta provide a refreshing change of pace. Visitors can take a scenic boat tour through the delta's waterways, visit local markets, or explore the riverside town. Boat tour prices vary, with most starting around ARS 1,000 per person.

2. **San Antonio de Areco** (www.areco.gob.ar): Located about 1.5 hours by car or bus from Buenos Aires, this picturesque town is known for its traditional gaucho (Argentine cowboy) culture. Visitors can explore the historic town center, visit estancias (ranches) for horseback riding, or attend the annual Fiesta de la Tradición. Prices for estancia visits and activities vary, starting from ARS 2,500 per person.

3. **Colonia del Sacramento, Uruguay** (www.colonia.gub.uy): A short ferry ride across the Río de la Plata takes visitors to the charming town of Colonia del Sacramento, a UNESCO World Heritage Site in Uruguay. With its cobblestone streets and well-preserved colonial architecture, Colonia makes for a perfect day trip or weekend getaway. Round-trip ferry tickets start at around ARS 3,500 per person, with discounts available when booking in advance.

4. **Luján** (www.lujan.gob.ar): Situated about 1.5 hours by car or bus from Buenos Aires, Luján is home to the famous Basilica de Nuestra Señora de Luján, an important pilgrimage site for Argentine Catholics. Visitors can also explore the colonial town center or visit the Enrique Udaondo Museum. Admission fees to museums and attractions typically range from ARS 200 to ARS 500.

5. La Plata (www.laplata.gob.ar): The capital city of Buenos Aires Province, La Plata is located just an hour by car or bus from the city. Highlights include the impressive La Plata Cathedral, the Natural Science Museum, and the Republica de los Niños theme park. Admission fees for museums and attractions typically range from ARS 200 to ARS 500.

VIII. Shopping

Here are some general tips about shopping in Buenos Aires:

- Clothes are much more expensive in Argentina when compared to Europe or USA. So, if you are coming from there, you will probably be rather shocked about the prices.
- You can find the main premium brands in any shopping mall, such as <u>Alto Palermo</u>, <u>Abasto</u>, <u>Galerías Pacífico</u>, or <u>Paseo Alcorta</u>.
- If you'd like to find lower prices, you have to head to Córdoba Avenue, within the Palermo neighborhood, where you will find lots of outlets. Most of these outlets are located right on Córdoba Avenue between the streets Lavalleja and Gurruchaga, which makes an extension of about 6 blocks full of outlets. On here you will find Levi's, Bowen, Kevingston or Kosiuko outlets, among others.

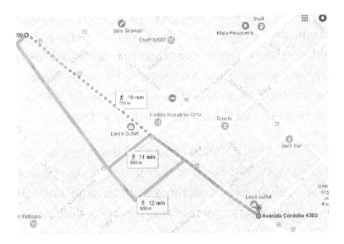

Get this map online: [Google Map] (https://bit.ly/3JowYql)

You will find another interesting outlet area over Aguirre Street between Serrano and Acevedo, within the Villa Crespo neighborhood, very close to the Córdoba Avenue outlets area.

Get this map online: [**Google Map**] (https://bit.ly/3Jom9Vo)

A. Shopping Centers and Malls

1. **Galerías Pacífico** (www.galeriaspacifico.com.ar): Located in the city center, this upscale shopping center is housed in a stunning Beaux-Arts building, featuring a variety of international brands, restaurants, and a food court.

2. **Patio Bullrich** (www.shoppingbullrich.com.ar): Situated in the Retiro neighborhood, Patio Bullrich is an elegant shopping mall offering high-end fashion brands, designer boutiques, and a refined dining experience.

3. **Alto Palermo** (www.altopalermo.com.ar): Located in the Palermo neighborhood, Alto Palermo is a popular shopping destination, featuring a wide range of fashion brands, electronics stores, and a large food court.

B. Local Markets and Artisan Fairs

1. **Feria de Mataderos** (www.feriademataderos.com.ar): This lively weekend fair in the Mataderos neighborhood showcases traditional

Argentine crafts, food, and live folk music. It's the perfect place to find unique souvenirs and experience local culture.

2. **Feria de San Telmo** (www.feriadesantelmo.com): Every Sunday, the cobblestone streets of San Telmo come alive with an antiques market and street fair, featuring handmade crafts, vintage items, and street performers.

3. **Feria de Plaza Francia**: Located in the Recoleta neighborhood, this weekend fair offers a variety of artisanal goods, including handmade jewelry, leather items, and traditional Argentine crafts.

C. Traditional Souvenirs and Gifts

1. **Calle Florida**: This bustling pedestrian street in the city center is lined with shops selling traditional Argentine products, such as leather goods, mate gourds, and tango music.

2. **Caminito** : In the colorful La Boca neighborhood, Caminito is a popular destination for tourists seeking hand-painted tango art, souvenirs, and Argentine crafts.

D. Luxury Shopping Districts

1. **Avenida Alvear**: Located in the upscale Recoleta neighborhood, Avenida Alvear is home to a number of luxury fashion boutiques, designer stores, and elegant hotels.

2. **Palermo Soho**: This trendy area of Palermo is known for its fashionable boutiques, designer shops, and hip cafés, making it a popular destination for those seeking stylish clothing, accessories, and home decor.

IX. Festivals and Events

Buenos Aires boasts a vibrant cultural scene, with numerous festivals and events taking place throughout the year. From traditional celebrations to contemporary arts and sporting events, there's always something happening in the city.

A. Annual Celebrations

Carnaval Porteño (www.buenosaires.gob.ar/carnaval): Taking place in February, this colorful street festival celebrates Argentine carnival traditions with murgas (percussion bands), costumed dancers, and lively parades across the city.

Fiesta Nacional del Tango: Held in December, this week-long celebration of tango features live music, dance performances, and tango workshops across various venues in Buenos Aires.

Día Nacional del Mate (www.yerbamateargentina.org.ar): On November 30th, Argentines celebrate their love for mate, the national drink, with events, tastings, and demonstrations throughout the city.

B. Film, Theater, and Music Festivals

Buenos Aires International Independent Film Festival (BAFICI) (www.buenosaires.gob.ar/festivales): Held annually in April, BAFICI showcases independent films from around the world, with screenings, workshops, and panel discussions.

Festival Internacional de Buenos Aires (FIBA) (www.buenosaires.gob.ar/festivalinternacional): This biennial performing arts festival, held in odd-numbered years, features international and Argentine theater, dance, and music performances at various venues across the city.

Buenos Aires Jazz Festival (www.buenosaires.gob.ar/festivalesdejazz): Taking place in November, this week-long festival celebrates jazz with concerts, jam sessions, and workshops featuring local and international artists.

C. Sporting Events

Argentine Open Polo Championship (www.aapolo.com): Held in November and December, this prestigious polo tournament attracts top international players and is hosted at the Campo Argentino de Polo in Palermo.

Buenos Aires Marathon (www.maratondebuenosaires.com): This annual 42-kilometer race takes place in September, drawing thousands of participants and spectators as it winds through the city's iconic landmarks and neighborhoods.

Buenos Aires ePrix (www.fiaformulae.com): This electric car racing event is part of the FIA Formula E Championship and takes place in Puerto Madero, showcasing cutting-edge technology and sustainability.

X. Practical Tips and Resources

A successful trip to Buenos Aires requires knowledge of some practical aspects of the city. Here are a few tips and resources to help you navigate language, communication, tipping etiquette, and staying connected during your visit.

A. Language and Communication

The official language in Buenos Aires is Spanish, but many locals, especially in tourist areas, speak English. Learning a few basic Spanish phrases can help enhance your experience and facilitate communication.

Helpful resources for learning Spanish include language apps like Duolingo (www.duolingo.com) and phrasebooks like Lonely Planet's Latin American Spanish Phrasebook & Dictionary.

B. Tipping Etiquette

In restaurants, it is customary to tip between 10% and 15% of the total bill. However, tipping is not obligatory, and the amount is up to your discretion based on the quality of service.

For hotel staff, such as bellhops and housekeeping, a small tip of around ARS 50 to ARS 100 is appreciated.

Taxi drivers do not generally expect tips, but rounding up to the nearest whole number or giving a small extra amount is a kind gesture.

C. Staying Connected: Wi-Fi and SIM Cards

Wi-Fi is widely available in Buenos Aires, with many hotels, cafés, and restaurants offering free access to their networks. The city also provides free public Wi-Fi in some parks and public spaces.

For a more reliable and secure connection, consider purchasing a local SIM card from one of Argentina's main mobile providers, such as Claro (www.claro.com.ar), Movistar (www.movistar.com.ar), or Personal (www.personal.com.ar). You will need to present your passport when purchasing a SIM card, and prepaid plans with data are available at a variety of prices.

D. Emergency Contacts and Services

In case of an emergency, dial 911 for immediate assistance from police, ambulance, or fire services.

The U.S. Embassy in Buenos Aires (https://ar.usembassy.gov) is located at Avenida Colombia 4300, and can provide assistance to U.S. citizens in case of emergencies or other issues.

It is advisable to research and note down the contact information for your country's embassy or consulate in Buenos Aires before your trip.

E. Useful Spanish Phrases

Even though Argentinians who deal with tourism usually speak some English, we suggest you learn some Spanish words before you head to Argentina, just in case.

As a traveler in Buenos Aires, it can be helpful to know some basic Spanish phrases to help you communicate with locals and get around the city. Here are some common phrases to use during your trip:

- Hola - Hello
- Buenos días - Good morning
- Buenas tardes - Good afternoon/evening
- Adiós - Goodbye
- Por favor - Please
- Gracias - Thank you
- De nada - You're welcome
- Lo siento - I'm sorry
- ¿Habla inglés? - Do you speak English?
- No hablo español - I don't speak Spanish
- ¿Cómo se dice... en español? - How do you say... in Spanish?
- ¿Dónde está...? - Where is...?
- ¿Cuánto cuesta? - How much does it cost?
- ¿Tiene...? - Do you have...?
- Me gustaría... - I would like...

Using these basic phrases can help you navigate your way around the city and communicate with locals. Many people in Buenos Aires speak at least some English, but making an effort to speak Spanish can be greatly appreciated and can help you connect with locals on a deeper level.

Additionally, learning a few basic phrases in Argentine Spanish can be useful, as the dialect has some unique differences from other varieties of Spanish. For example, in Argentine Spanish, the pronoun "you" is often replaced with "vos" instead of "tu," and there are many local slang words and phrases that are unique to the region.

Overall, using some basic Spanish phrases during your trip to Buenos Aires can help you connect with locals and enhance your overall travel experience. Don't be afraid to try out your Spanish, even if it's not perfect - the effort will be appreciated and can go a long way in making new friends and discovering new places.

Common Greetings in Spanish

English Word	Spanish Word	Pronunciation
Good morning.	Buenos días.	booEHN-os DEE-as
Good afternoon.	Buenas tardes.	booEHN-as TAR-dehs
Good evening	Buenas Noches.	booEHN-as NO-chehs
Hello, my name is John	Hola, me llamo Juan.	OH-la meh YA-mo Wahn
What is your name?	¿Cómo te llamas?	KOH-moh teh YA-mahs
How are you?	¿Cómo estás?	KOH-moh ehs-TAS
I am fine.	Estoy bien.	ehs-TOY bee-EHN
Nice to meet you.	Mucho gusto.	MOO-choh GOOS-toh
Goodbye.	Adiós.	ah-dee-OHS
See you later.	Hasta luego.	AHS-ta looEH-go
Please.	Por favor.	pohr fah-VOR
Thank you.	Gracias.	gra-SEE-ahs
You are welcome	De nada.	deh NA-da

The Numbers in Spanish

1	Uno	oo-no
2	Dos	Dose
3	Tres	Trace
4	Cuatro	Kwat-ro
5	Cinco	Sink-o
6	Seis	Saze
7	Siete	See-yet-eh
8	Ocho	Och-o
9	Nueve	New-eh-veh
10	Diez	Dee-ace
20	Veinte	Bayn-tay
30	Treinta	Trayn-tah
40	Cuarenta	Kwah-rayn-tah
50	Cincuenta	Seen-kwayn-tah
60	Sesenta	Say-sayn-tah
70	Setenta	Say-tayn-tah
80	Ochenta	Oh-chayn-tah
90	Noventa	Noh-bayn-tah
100	Cien	Syehn

Thank you.Gracias.	Hi. Hola	Yes. Sí.	Good morning. Buenos días
You're welcome. De nada.	I want. Yo quiero	No. No.	Good afternoon. Buenas tardes
Please. Por favor.	I want a taxi. Yo quiero un taxi.	Here. Aqui.	Good evening. Buenas noches
Excuse me. Con permiso.	I want a beer. Yo quiero una cerveza.	There. Alli	I'm sorry. Lo siento.
Pardon me. Perdone.	I don't want. Yo no quiero	Street. La Calle.	I don't understand. No entiendo.

Who? Quien?	How? Como?	Right. A la derecho	I don't speak Spanish. No hablo español.
What? Que?	How much? Cuanto?	Left . A la izquierda	Do you speak English? Habla inglés?
Where? Donde?	How many? Cuantos?	Straight ahead. Derecho	What's your name? Cómo se llama?
When? Cuando?	How long? Por cuanto tiempo?	Where is the bank? Dónde está el banco?	My name is ... Me llamo...
Why? Por que?	How are you? Cómo está?	Where is the subway? Dónde está el metro?	What time is it? Qué hora es?

At the Restaurant

A table – **Una mesa**	A menu – **Un menu**	Soup – **Sopa**
Salad – **Ensalada**	Burger – **Hamburguesa**	An appetizer – **Una entrada**
Dessert – **Un postre**	A drink – **Una bebida**	Water – **Agua**
Red wine– **Vino tinto**	White Wine - **vino blanco**	Beer – **Cerveza**
Chicken. El pollo	**The meat. La carne**	**Water. Una agua**

What do you recommend? Que me recomienda?	I am vegetarian. Soy vegetariano/a	I have allergy to .. Tengo alergia a ...
Coffee – Un café	(Calling a waiter if he is a man): Senor!	(Calling a waitress): Senorita!
The check – La cuenta (e.g. Senor, la cuenta por favor)	Is the tip included? Incluye la propina?	How much does that cost? Cuánto cuesta?
Where is the bathroom? Dónde está el baño?		

3-Day Itinerary: Classic Buenos Aires

Welcome to Buenos Aires, the vibrant capital of Argentina, often referred to as the "Paris of South America." This bustling city is known for its rich culture, stunning architecture, passionate tango, and mouth-watering cuisine. Our carefully curated 3-day itinerary offers you the chance to explore the city's classic attractions and immerse yourself in the authentic porteño lifestyle. From iconic landmarks and charming neighborhoods to tango shows and traditional parrillas, this guide will help you make the most of your time in this enchanting city. Let's dive into the magic of Buenos Aires!

1st Day In Buenos Aires - Itinerary

9:00

Arrival at Ezeiza (EZE) / Ministro Pistarini International Airport, which is 22 km away from the city center

Ezeiza International Airport (EZE) is the main international airport serving Buenos Aires, Argentina. It is located about 22 kilometers (13.7 miles) from the city center and is a hub for many international airlines.

Here are some tips to help travelers navigate EZE airport:

- Allow plenty of time: As with any international airport, it's important to arrive early to allow time for check-in, security, and boarding. It is recommended that passengers arrive at EZE airport at least three hours before their scheduled departure time.
- Have your documents ready: Make sure you have your passport, boarding pass, and any other necessary documents ready for check-in and security. Check the visa requirements for your destination country before you travel.
- Plan your transportation: There are several transportation options available from EZE airport to the city center, including taxi, shuttle bus, and public transportation. Consider the time of day, traffic, and your budget when choosing your transportation.

- Familiarize yourself with the airport layout: EZE airport has three terminals, and it's important to know which terminal your flight departs from. You can check your terminal on your boarding pass or by contacting your airline.
- Take advantage of airport amenities: EZE airport offers a variety of amenities for travelers, including duty-free shopping, restaurants, cafes, and lounges. Make sure you have Argentine pesos or a credit card to make purchases.
- Stay connected: EZE airport offers free Wi-Fi throughout the terminal, so you can stay connected to family and friends or catch up on work.
- Be aware of customs regulations: Argentina has strict customs regulations, and it's important to declare any items that may be restricted or prohibited. Be aware of the limits on duty-free purchases and alcohol and tobacco allowances.

By following these tips, travelers can navigate EZE airport with ease and make their trip to Buenos Aires a smooth and enjoyable experience.

9:30

Take an official airport taxi to the city center, Palermo or Recoleta, which are our recommended neighborhoods for your stay in Buenos Aires.

Cost: 20€ *Taxi*

10:30

Arrival at the hotel. Accommodate yourself and rest for a little while before starting your first day getting to know Buenos Aires!

11:30

We recommend taking the **Hop-on-Hop-Off Bus** during your first day in Buenos Aires, even if normally we're not really fans of this kind of coaches to be honest. The thing is that Buenos Aires is a huge city, with several different neighborhoods very different from one another, and distances are not very walkable sometimes. We believe that taking the Hop-on-Hop-off Bus at your first day can give you a first impression of all of the different neighborhoods so that you make an idea. Some of the neighborhoods that you get to know while riding on this bus are **Monserrat, San Telmo, La Boca, Puerto Madero, Retiro, Recoleta, Belgrano, and Palermo**. If you're staying in Buenos Aires, there is no way you can get to know and see all of these neighborhoods by yourself without taking a bus like this one, and that is why we recommend it for your first day.

You can also get off at any of its 33 stops, walk around, and then catch the next bus 30 minutes later. Take into account that on this guide we will be proposing specific visits to Palermo, Recoleta, San Telmo and La Boca for the following days, so maybe you can avoid getting off at those stops since you will get to know them later anyway. The bus ticket includes an audio-guide so that you can hear some interesting facts about these neighborhoods' rich history. Tickets cost around 33€ per person, and you can get them in advance here.

Our recommendation is to go from the hotel to the **Obelisk** so you can see Buenos Aires' **most famous monument**. At this time of the day, you will also be able to see how the heart of this city looks like during daytime, with thousands of people walking around. Then you can take the **Hop-on-Hop-off Bus** from the Obelisk and start your tour.

Cost: 33€ Hop-on-Hop-off Bus

Casa Rosada

After your first impression of Buenos Aires and all of its different neighborhoods with the Hop-on-Hop-off Bus, we recommend getting to know a bit more about **the center of the city and its historical parts**.

National Congress Palace

You may start at the **National Congress Palace**; this is where Avenida de Mayo begins, which extends to **Plaza de Mayo**, one of the most iconic places in the city. At Plaza de Mayo you will also be able to see the **Casa Rosada**, which is the seat of the National Government. During this 2 km walk, you will be able to see all the most emblematic and historical places and buildings of Buenos Aires history. See *ZoomTip 1.1* to know more about the importance of these sites.

Get this map online: [**Google Map**] (https://bit.ly/46oPDfI)

18:30

Following an exhilarating first day, return to your hotel for some well-deserved downtime before your evening meal. Keep in mind that dinner in Buenos Aires typically starts no earlier than 9 PM to 9:30 PM. Given that we have exciting plans for your first night, we suggest you take advantage of this interim period to relax and recharge, preparing yourself for the upcoming evening activities.

20:45

For your first night, we recommend indulging in Argentina's renowned steak at a local parrilla. As previously suggested, **La Cabrera,** located at 5127 Cabrera Street, comes highly recommended. Alternatively, you might consider visiting **Don Julio** at 4691 Guatemala Street or El 22 at 1950 Carranza Street. These establishments offer exceptional culinary experiences that are sure to delight.

Cost: 25€ approx. *Parrilla Dinner*

22:30

To cap off an incredible first day in Buenos Aires, we suggest immersing yourself in the city's vibrant tango scene. Experience live music and captivating performances in the very neighborhoods where this iconic dance style originated. The intersection of San Juan and Boedo in the Boedo district is considered the heart of Buenos Aires' tango culture. Alternatively, the Abasto neighborhood offers other notable venues such as La Catedral, located at 4006 Sarmiento Street, an antique-filled warehouse turned tango haven. Another option is La Viruta at 1366 Armenia Street, where you can both dance and watch others sway to the rhythm of tango for hours. After 2 AM, professional dancers take the floor, providing you with the opportunity to sit back, relax, and marvel at their expertise.

1st Day in Buenos Aires - Map

Below you will find the maps corresponding to all the different activities that we recommend for your first day in Buenos Aires. They are accessible in Google Maps format for you to easily use on your smartphone or tablet while you are in Buenos Aires.

As you can see on the map, a significant part of the city is covered on your first day, mainly thanks to the hop-on-hop-off bus.

Get this map online: [**Google Map**] (https://bit.ly/3Jgdog4). You can download all the Google Maps for Buenos Aires so as to have offline

access. Here is some information on how to do it:
https://blog.google/products/maps/google-maps-offline/

ZoomTip 1.1: 1st Day Monuments
Obelisk

The Obelisk is one of the most iconic landmarks in Buenos Aires, and it is a must-visit destination for anyone traveling to the city. The monument stands at the intersection of two major avenues in the city center, Avenida 9 de Julio and Avenida Corrientes, and it is one of the most recognizable symbols of Buenos Aires.

The Obelisk was built in 1936 to commemorate the 400th anniversary of the city's founding. It stands at a height of 67.5 meters (221 feet) and is made of concrete and stone. The monument is visible from many different parts of the city, and it has become a popular meeting spot for locals and tourists alike.

The Obelisk is often used as a backdrop for festivals, concerts, and other public events in Buenos Aires. It has also been featured in several movies, including the famous tango scene in the movie "Evita."

The area around the Obelisk is bustling with activity, with many shops, cafes, and restaurants nearby. It is also home to several important landmarks, including the Teatro Colón, one of the world's most famous opera houses, and the Plaza de la República, a large public square.

Overall, the Obelisk is a must-see destination for anyone visiting Buenos Aires. Its iconic shape and central location make it a perfect spot to capture some memorable photos or simply take in the vibrant energy of the city.

National Congress Palace

The National Congress Palace (Palacio del Congreso Nacional) is a stunning neoclassical building located in the heart of Buenos Aires. It is the seat of the Argentine National Congress and is a must-visit destination for anyone interested in Argentine history and politics.

The National Congress Palace was designed by the Italian architect Vittorio Meano and the Argentine architect Julio Dormal. Construction began in 1898 and was completed in 1906. The building is characterized by its impressive dome, which stands at a height of 80 meters (262 feet) and is covered in copper sheets.

The palace has a grand entrance hall, lined with statues and frescoes that depict significant moments in Argentine history. The building also houses several libraries, a museum, and a chamber for meetings of the National Congress.

One of the most interesting facts about the National Congress Palace is that it was built using materials and resources from all over Argentina. The marble used for the interior was sourced from the province of

Córdoba, the bronze statues were cast in the province of Entre Rios, and the wooden panels in the library were made from the native quebracho tree.

Another interesting fact is that the building was designed to be earthquake-proof, as the architects wanted to ensure the safety of the National Congress and its members in the event of a seismic event.

Visitors to the National Congress Palace can take guided tours of the building, which provide insights into Argentine politics and history. The tours include visits to the various halls and chambers, as well as the library and museum.

Overall, the National Congress Palace is an impressive and important landmark in Buenos Aires, and it is a must-visit destination for anyone interested in Argentine politics and history. The stunning architecture and interesting facts make it a fascinating and educational experience for visitors of all ages.

Casa Rosada

Casa Rosada, also known as the Pink House, is the presidential palace of Argentina, located in the Plaza de Mayo in Buenos Aires. It is a beautiful and iconic landmark of the city, and it has played an important role in Argentine history and politics.

The palace was originally built in the 16th century as a customs house, and it was later used as the headquarters of the Argentine government.

The distinctive pink color of the building comes from a mixture of lime and ox blood, which was used in the construction of the palace.

One of the most interesting facts about Casa Rosada is that it has been the site of many important events in Argentine history. The balcony of the palace, known as the balcony of Eva Perón, was the site of many of the speeches given by Eva Perón, the wife of President Juan Perón, and a prominent figure in Argentine politics and culture.

Visitors to Casa Rosada can take a guided tour of the palace, which includes visits to the various rooms and halls, as well as the museum and art gallery. One of the most impressive rooms is the Hall of Argentine Independence, which features beautiful frescoes and stained glass windows depicting important moments in Argentine history.

The palace is surrounded by beautiful gardens, which offer a peaceful escape from the busy city streets. Visitors can enjoy a stroll through the gardens and take in the beautiful architecture of the palace from outside.

Casa Rosada is an important and iconic landmark of Buenos Aires, and it is a must-visit destination for anyone interested in Argentine history and politics. The palace offers a fascinating glimpse into the country's past and present, and the beautiful architecture and gardens make it a memorable and picturesque experience for visitors.

Plaza de Mayo

Most of the more important moments in the history of Argentina happened at *Plaza de Mayo*. The city's founder, Juan de Garay, planted the symbol of justice here on 1580. Since then, *Plaza de Mayo* became the center of the citizens' life, where the most severe acts and celebrations occurred.

Plaza de Mayo is where the famous *Madres de Plaza de Mayo* gathered every Thursday since April of 1977, with signs and pictures of their *disappeared* sons and daughters during the military coup that terrified the city and the entire country during that time.

2nd Day In Buenos Aires – Itinerary

9:00

Visit *La Boca*.

Make sure to explore La Boca, one of Buenos Aires' most vibrant neighborhoods. The heart of this area is Caminito, a pedestrian-only street spanning just 100 meters, adorned with small, multicolored buildings that uniquely lack front doors. As a popular tourist destination, the surrounding streets are bustling with tango dancers, restaurants, and gift shops. However, these tend to be significantly pricier compared to other parts of the city, so we advise against making any major purchases here.

Once you've explored Caminito and its surroundings, we suggest a visit to the Quinquela Martin Museum, home to one of the most extensive collections of Argentinian art from the late 19th century to the present day. The museum is quite compact, so a little over an hour should suffice for your visit. Following the museum, take a leisurely stroll along the riverbank towards La Bombonera, the legendary stadium of Boca Juniors. This iconic football stadium is among the most renowned worldwide. If you're a football enthusiast, consider taking a guided tour of the Boca Juniors Museum, available for a modest fee of 10 €.

La Bombonera, nestled in Buenos Aires' La Boca neighborhood, is the celebrated home of Boca Juniors, one of the world's most iconic football teams. The stadium's distinctive architecture, with one end curving inward, resembles a box of chocolates, earning it the nickname "La Bombonera," or "the chocolate box."

For football enthusiasts, a trip to La Bombonera is an essential part of the Buenos Aires experience. Guided tours offer a deep dive into the history of the team and the stadium, including a visit to the Boca Juniors museum, which showcases the team's storied past and its legendary players.

The tour's pinnacle is a visit to the stadium itself, where you can witness the fervor of "La Doce" (The Twelfth), the team's fan group, as they cheer from the stands. Experience the thrill of walking through the tunnel leading to the field, imagining the sensation of stepping onto the pitch amid the roar of thousands of ardent fans.

If you're fortunate enough to be in Buenos Aires during a Boca Juniors home game, attending a match at La Bombonera is an experience you won't forget. Known for its electrifying atmosphere, the stadium reverberates with the sound of fans singing and chanting throughout the game. The Boca Juniors fans are renowned for their unwavering passion and loyalty, creating an unparalleled level of support for their team.

Beyond the stadium, the vibrant La Boca neighborhood awaits exploration, with its brightly colored houses and captivating street art. The area is dotted with restaurants and cafes, offering the perfect spots to savor a traditional Argentine meal or a cup of coffee while soaking up the local culture.

In summary, a visit to La Bombonera is a must for football fans and those interested in Argentine culture. As an integral part of Buenos Aires' identity, the stadium's unique architecture and passionate fans make it an unforgettable destination.

Cost: 10€ La Bombonera

Visit San Telmo.

Following your exploration of La Boca, it's time to experience the charm of its neighboring district, San Telmo. Given that La Boca isn't entirely safe for pedestrians outside its main tourist areas, we recommend taking a taxi to San Telmo. The short distance ensures the fare will be reasonable.

Upon arrival in San Telmo, begin your adventure at the district's heart: Plaza Dorrego. This bustling square is teeming with eateries, musicians, and lively energy. If you visit on a weekend, you'll have the opportunity to explore the remarkable San Telmo Market, a treasure trove of antiques, toys, vintage Argentinian items, and much more. While the market is open daily, a significant portion of it is closed on weekdays, so for the full experience, we recommend a Saturday or Sunday visit.

After grabbing a bite in Plaza Dorrego or one of the picturesque streets of San Telmo, consider a visit to the Modern Arts Museum. Located just a few blocks from Plaza Dorrego at 350 San Juan Avenue, the museum offers an extensive collection of contemporary art. The entrance fee is a mere 1.5€, making it an affordable and enriching cultural experience.

Following your museum visit, we suggest a leisurely stroll to **Parque Lezama**. This beautiful park offers a tranquil respite from the city's hustle and bustle, allowing you to immerse yourself in a bit of nature amidst the urban landscape.

Cost: 1.5€ *Museum of Modern Arts Entrance*

Explore Puerto Madero.

Once you've soaked in the charm of San Telmo, we suggest a 15-minute walk to Puerto Madero. This district is the epitome of modernity in Buenos Aires, marked by towering skyscrapers. The architectural contrast between San Telmo and Puerto Madero is striking, despite their close proximity. Here, you can savor a stunning sunset, providing a perfect conclusion to your day. Additionally, enjoy a leisurely stroll through its serene, contemporary streets. Given the usual bustle of Buenos Aires, the tranquility of Puerto Madero's roads offers a unique and peaceful experience.

19:30

After your day of exploration, head back to your hotel for some relaxation and dinner. We suggest sampling the renowned Argentinian empanadas, which you can find at numerous eateries within a short walk from your hotel. Alternatively, refer to the "Where To Find The Best Empanadas In Buenos Aires" chapter in this guide for more detailed recommendations.

Enjoy Palermo's nightlife.

After dinner, consider experiencing the vibrant nightlife of Palermo with a nighttime stroll through this picturesque neighborhood. Palermo, a large district divided into several sections including Palermo Viejo, Palermo Chico, and Palermo Hollywood, is known for its lively bar scene. We recommend starting your night tour in Palermo Viejo, with its charming streets and eclectic bars.

Kick off your evening at Shanghai Dragon, located at 1197 Aráoz Street. This oriental-themed bar offers a wide selection of craft beers in a unique setting. After savoring a beer or two at Shanghai Dragon, take a walk around Plaza Serrano, the heart of Palermo Viejo, and explore its enchanting side streets.

While Plaza Serrano is surrounded by numerous bars, many cater primarily to tourists and can be quite pricey. However, just a couple of blocks away, you'll find a hidden gem: Soria Bar at 5151 Gorriti Street. This bar boasts a spacious garden, creating a comfortable atmosphere that attracts a diverse crowd from around the world. While their beer selection is limited to well-known brands, their cocktails are expertly crafted and reasonably priced. It's a great spot to share stories about your Buenos Aires adventures with fellow travelers.

If you're still brimming with energy and eager to continue exploring, carry on walking along **Gorriti Street** towards **Palermo Hollywood**. This area gets its name from the numerous television channels and film studios located here, so don't be surprised if you spot a few famous faces in the local bars. We recommend a visit to **Carnal,** located at 5511 Niceto Vega Avenue.

For those ready to dive into the vibrant nightlife, **Niceto Club** is conveniently situated right across the street. This club, open until 6 AM, showcases some of the best new alternative music scenes. Live bands perform until 3 AM, followed by DJ sets that keep the party going until dawn. It's the perfect spot for night owls looking to experience Buenos Aires' dynamic music scene.

2nd Day in Buenos Aires - Map

Below you will find the maps corresponding to all the different activities that we recommend for your second day in Buenos Aires. They are accessible in Google Maps format for you to easily use on your smartphone or tablet while you are in Buenos Aires.

We've divided this day into two different maps: one corresponds to your time itinerary (La Boca, San Telmo, and Puerto Madero), and the second one corresponds to your night plan (Palermo at night).

Day Itinerary Map:

Get this map online here: [Google Map] (https://bit.ly/43MaHLk)

SCAN ME

You can download all the Google Maps for Buenos Aires so as to have offline access. Here is some information on how to do it:

https://blog.google/products/maps/google-maps-offline/

Night Itinerary Map:

Get this map online: [**Google Map**] (https://bit.ly/43LOmot)

ZoomTip 2.1: Information on Buenos Aires Modern Arts Museum

Buenos Aires Modern Arts Museum (http://museomoderno.net **)** (usually referred as MOMBA) opened on 1956 and has been one of the most important museums of the city ever since, along with the famous MALBA (Latin American Arts Museum of Buenos Aires). Entrance is 30 pesos and free for students.

The Modern Arts Entrance (El Museo de Arte Moderno de Buenos Aires) is a contemporary art museum located in the San Telmo neighborhood of Buenos Aires. The museum features a collection of modern and contemporary art from both Argentine and international artists.

The museum's entrance is a striking piece of modern architecture that was designed by the Argentine architect Emilio Ambasz. The building features a large, curved facade made of glass and concrete, which is both functional and visually impressive.

Once inside, visitors can explore the museum's collection, which includes paintings, sculptures, installations, and other contemporary art forms. The museum regularly hosts temporary exhibitions and installations, as well as cultural events and performances.

Here are some of the top exhibits to see at the Modern Arts Entrance:

- **The permanent collection:** The museum's permanent collection features works by some of the most influential Argentine artists of the 20th century, including Antonio Berni, Xul Solar, and Eduardo Mac Entyre. The collection also includes works by international artists such as Pablo Picasso, Wassily Kandinsky, and Henry Moore.
- **Julio Le Parc's "Lumière":** This exhibit features the work of the Argentine kinetic artist Julio Le Parc, who is known for his use of light and movement in his art. The exhibit includes a variety of installations and sculptures that use light and color to create immersive and interactive experiences for visitors.
- **Leandro Erlich's "Construction Site":** This installation by the Argentine artist Leandro Erlich is a fascinating commentary on the construction industry and its impact on urban environments. The installation features a simulated construction site with a series of mirrors that create the illusion of a vertical tunnel.
- **The museum cafe:** The museum's cafe is a unique and artistic space that offers a great view of the surrounding San Telmo neighborhood. The cafe features a rotating selection of artwork and a menu of Argentine and international cuisine.
- **The museum shop:** The museum shop offers a great selection of contemporary art books, posters, and other unique items. It's a great place to find a souvenir or a unique gift.

Overall, the Modern Arts Entrance is a fascinating destination for anyone interested in contemporary art and architecture. Its unique entrance and impressive collection of works make it a must-visit destination for anyone traveling to Buenos Aires.

Address: Av. San Juan 350, C1147AAO CABA, Argentina| Open Hours: Monday Closed, Tuesday to Friday from 11 to 18:30, Saturday and Sunday from 11 to 20:00.| Founded: 1956| Tel: +54 11 4361-6919

Google Arts Projects: https://artsandculture.google.com/partner/museo-de-arte-moderno-de-buenos-aires-museo-moderno

09:00

Check out from the hotel, deposit your luggage there and go to Teatro Colón

On your final day in Buenos Aires, we recommend starting with a visit to the historic **Colón Theatre**. This iconic venue is regarded as one of the world's finest theaters, and its grandeur becomes immediately apparent upon entering. Opt for the guided tour, which departs every 15 minutes, to fully appreciate its architectural and cultural significance. For more detailed information about the Colón Theatre, refer to ZoomTip 3.1 in this guide.

Cost: *Colón Theatre Tour* 13€

11:00

Take the metro and head to the Chinese neighborhood in Belgrano.

Following your visit to the historic Colón Theatre, we recommend extending your day's adventure to **Buenos Aires' Chinatown.** Like any other Chinatown around the world, you'll discover a wealth of intriguing sights and beautifully adorned streets, offering a unique cultural experience within the city.

The Chinese neighborhood in **Belgrano**, also known as **Barrio Chino**, is a vibrant and bustling area of Buenos Aires that is home to a large Chinese community. The neighborhood is centered **around Arribeños and Juramento streets** in the Belgrano district, and it is a popular destination for locals and tourists alike.

The Chinese community in Belgrano has a rich history in Buenos Aires, dating back to the 1980s when the first wave of Chinese immigrants began to settle in the area. Over the years, the neighborhood has grown to become one of the largest and most vibrant Chinese communities in South America.

Visitors to Barrio Chino can enjoy a variety of sights, sounds, and flavors. The neighborhood is famous for its many Chinese shops, restaurants, and markets, which offer a range of goods and delicacies from China and other parts of Asia.

One of the most popular attractions in Barrio Chino is the annual Chinese New Year festival, which takes place in late January or early February. The festival features a variety of traditional Chinese performances, such as dragon and lion dances, as well as food stalls and cultural exhibits.

In addition to the Chinese community, Barrio Chino is also home to a number of Japanese, Korean, and other Asian businesses, adding to the area's diverse and multicultural atmosphere.

Overall, the Chinese neighborhood in Belgrano is a unique and fascinating destination in Buenos Aires. Whether you're looking for delicious food, cultural experiences, or a glimpse into one of the city's most vibrant communities, Barrio Chino is definitely worth a visit.

After this, you can take a little walk around the **Belgrano** neighborhood, where you will find some beautiful architecture (walk a bit through *Cabildo Avenue*), and you'll see lots of typical *porteños* through their routines.

If you're a football fan, here you're close to **El Monumental**, which is River Plate's stadium. *River Plate* and *Boca Juniors* are the two most important football teams in Argentina by far; and *El Monumental* is the biggest football stadium in the nation and is the home of the **Argentinian National Team**, even though *La Bombonera* is more famous due to its history and its original design.

You can have something for lunch here at Belgrano neighborhood if you're hungry. There are dozens of different places to eat you will come across while walking around.

Take a walk through the Palermo Forests

The immense neighborhood of Palermo has a vast area of beautiful forests for you to enjoy. We recommend starting at the **Jardín Japonés** (Japanese Garden), which is a gorgeous space full of life. It is one of the largest Japanese gardens of its type outside of Japan. The price of entrance is only 5€.

After your visit to the Japanese Garden, continue walking through the forests and go to **Galileo Galilei Planetarium**. If you choose to enter the place, you can see a piece of lunar rock or 100 million years old sea life fossils, among many other things. If you're not that interested, you can simply walk around the beautiful surrounding park.

The Galileo Galilei Planetarium is a world-class observatory and planetarium located in the Palermo neighborhood of Buenos Aires. The building was designed by Argentine architect Enrique Jan and opened in 1966, making it one of the oldest and most iconic landmarks in the city.

The planetarium offers a range of exhibits and attractions, including a state-of-the-art planetarium theater, a museum, and a digital dome. Here are some of the top things to see at the Galileo Galilei Planetarium:

- Planetarium theater: The planetarium's theater is the largest in Latin America and features a 360-degree dome that offers an immersive and unforgettable experience. Visitors can enjoy a variety of shows and presentations, including live music performances and multimedia shows that explore the mysteries of the universe.
- Museum: The planetarium's museum features exhibits on astronomy, space exploration, and the history of the planetarium itself. Visitors can learn about the planets, stars, and galaxies, as well as the technology and techniques used by astronomers to explore the universe.
- Digital dome: The planetarium's digital dome offers a unique and interactive experience that uses cutting-edge technology to simulate space and the cosmos. Visitors can explore the universe in stunning detail and learn about the latest discoveries in space science.
- Observatory: The planetarium also houses an observatory that is open to the public on selected nights. Visitors can observe the stars

and planets through telescopes and learn about the constellations and other astronomical phenomena.

- Garden: The planetarium's garden is a beautiful and tranquil space that offers a peaceful retreat from the city. It features a variety of native and exotic plant species, as well as sculptures and other art installations.

Overall, the Galileo Galilei Planetarium is a fascinating destination in Buenos Aires that offers a unique and immersive experience for anyone interested in space and astronomy. Its world-class facilities and exhibits make it a must-visit destination for science enthusiasts and anyone looking to expand their knowledge of the universe.

Here is some visitor information for the Galileo Galilei Planetarium in Buenos Aires:

Location: The planetarium is located in the Palermo neighborhood of Buenos Aires, at Av. Sarmiento and Av. Figueroa Alcorta. It is easily accessible by public transportation, including bus and subway.

Hours: The planetarium is open from Tuesday to Sunday, from 1 pm to 7 pm. It is closed on Mondays and certain holidays.

Tickets: Admission to the planetarium is ticketed, and visitors can purchase tickets at the planetarium or online. Prices vary depending on the type of show or exhibit, with discounts available for children, students, and senior citizens.

Languages: Most exhibits and shows at the planetarium are available in Spanish, but some also have translations in English and other languages. Visitors can check with the planetarium staff for details.

Accessibility: The planetarium is wheelchair accessible and has facilities for people with disabilities. Visitors with special needs can contact the planetarium in advance to arrange for any necessary accommodations.

Guided tours: Guided tours of the planetarium are available in Spanish and English, and can be arranged in advance by contacting the planetarium staff.

Other information: Visitors should be aware that the planetarium may be crowded during peak hours, such as weekends and holidays. It is recommended to arrive early to avoid long lines and ensure availability of preferred shows or exhibits. Visitors should also be aware that flash photography is not permitted inside the planetarium.

16:00

Visit Recoleta neighborhood.

For the final hours of your Buenos Aires journey, we suggest immersing yourself in the stunning Recoleta neighborhood. Often likened to Paris, this district is arguably the most European part of the city.

The neighborhood's crown jewel is the **Recoleta Cemetery**, a renowned landmark recognized by the likes of BBC and CNN as one of the world's most beautiful cemeteries. We recommend a visit to this extraordinary open-air museum, where you can appreciate its historical and architectural significance.

Recoleta Cemetery is one of the most famous landmarks in Buenos Aires, and one of the most iconic cemeteries in the world. It is located in the upscale Recoleta neighborhood, and is the final resting place of many of Argentina's most notable and influential figures.

The cemetery was established in 1822, and is known for its impressive architecture, sculptures, and mausoleums. Over the years, it has become a popular destination for visitors interested in history, culture, and art.

Many of Argentina's most famous and influential figures are buried in Recoleta Cemetery, including former presidents, military leaders, artists, and intellectuals. Here are some of the most notable figures buried in the cemetery:

- **Eva Perón:** Eva Perón, also known as Evita, was one of Argentina's most beloved and controversial figures. She was the second wife of former President Juan Perón, and was known for her work on behalf of the poor and marginalized. Her tomb in Recoleta Cemetery is one of the most visited and iconic sites in the cemetery.
- **Domingo Faustino Sarmiento:** Sarmiento was a writer, educator, and politician who served as President of Argentina from 1868 to 1874. He is considered one of the most important figures in Argentine history, and his tomb in Recoleta Cemetery is a popular destination for visitors.
- **Rufina Cambaceres:** Cambaceres was a socialite and member of one of Argentina's most prominent families. Her untimely death at a young age inspired a legend that she was buried alive, and her tomb in Recoleta Cemetery is known for its striking and haunting design.
- **Carlos Gardel:** Gardel was an iconic tango singer and actor who is often referred to as the "King of Tango." His tomb in Recoleta Cemetery is a popular destination for fans of his music, and is known for its striking and unique design.

Overall, Recoleta Cemetery is a fascinating and unique destination in Buenos Aires, and a must-visit for anyone interested in history, culture, or art. Its impressive architecture and sculptures, as well as the notable figures buried within, make it a truly special and unforgettable site.

Take your luggage and head to the airport.

Enjoy a leisurely stroll through the picturesque streets of Recoleta, savor a cup of coffee at one of its charming cafes, and reflect on the remarkable experiences you've had during your three-day stay in Buenos Aires. It's the perfect way to bid farewell to this vibrant city before you embark on your journey home.

3d Day in Buenos Aires – Map

Below you will find the map corresponding to all the different activities that we recommend for your second day in Buenos Aires. They are accessible in Google Maps format for you to easily use on your smartphone or tablet while you are in Buenos Aires.

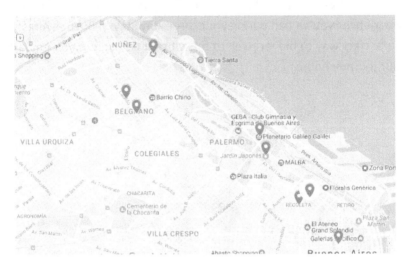

Get this map online: [**Google Map**] (https://bit.ly/3CyFI9y)

SCAN ME

You can download all the Google Maps for Buenos Aires so as to have offline access. Here is some information on how to do it:

https://blog.google/products/maps/google-maps-offline/

ZoomTip 3.1: Colón Theatre

The **Colón Theatre** is the main opera house in Buenos Aires. It is currently ranked as the 3rd best opera house in the whole world by National Geographic, and also considered among the best five in the world regarding acoustic.

The original theater opened in 1857 and was replaced by a new theater that took a 20-years construction and opened in 1908.

Teatro Colon is one of the most prestigious and beautiful opera houses in the world. Located in the heart of Buenos Aires, it is a must-visit destination for anyone who loves music, architecture, and history.

The opera house was designed by Italian architect Francesco Tamburini and Argentine architect Victor Meano, and opened in 1908. It has since undergone several renovations and restorations, with the most recent one being completed in 2010.

The interior of Teatro Colon is stunning, with ornate details and rich colors throughout. The auditorium features four levels of seating and a stunning ceiling painting, "The Chariot of Apollo," by Argentine artist Raul Soldi. The theater also has a spectacular chandelier made of Bohemian crystal, which weighs over one ton.

Teatro Colon is known for its impressive acoustics, which are some of the best in the world. The theater has hosted many of the most renowned musicians and singers of the 20th and 21st centuries, including Maria Callas, Placido Domingo, and Luciano Pavarotti.

Visitors can take a guided tour of the opera house, which includes visits to the main hall, stage, and backstage areas. The tour provides a fascinating insight into the history and workings of the theater, as well as some of its most important performances and events.

In addition to operas, Teatro Colon hosts a wide variety of concerts and events throughout the year, including ballets, symphonies, and recitals. It is also home to a ballet company, the Ballet Estable, which performs regularly at the theater.

Overall, Teatro Colon is a magnificent destination in Buenos Aires, and a must-visit for anyone who appreciates music, history, and architecture. Its stunning beauty and impressive acoustics make it one of the world's most renowned opera houses, and a true gem of Argentine culture.

Tip: If you want to skip the lines and experience a more private tour of Colon Theater, try the Buenos Aires: Skip-the-Line Colon Theater and Palaces Tour (https://bit.ly/46nk4D0)

Thank You!

Buenos Aires is a city that offers a unique blend of history, culture, and entertainment. With its stunning architecture, delicious food, and friendly locals, it's no wonder that it's one of the most popular travel destinations in South America.

We hope this guide has been helpful in planning your trip to Buenos Aires and has provided you with some valuable information on the city's top attractions, must-see sights, and local culture.

Remember, Buenos Aires is a city that rewards exploration, and the best experiences are often the ones that you stumble upon by chance. So take your time, soak up the local atmosphere, and immerse yourself in all that this wonderful city has to offer.

Thank you for choosing Buenos Aires as your travel destination, and we wish you a safe and memorable trip.

Have an amazing time in Buenos Aires!

Your friends at Guidora.

Copyright Notice
Guidora Buenos Aires in 3 Days Travel Guide ©

Disclaimer

The publishers have checked the information in this travel guide, but its accuracy is not warranted or guaranteed. Buenos Aires visitors are advised that opening times should always be checked before making a journey.

Tracing Copyright Owners

Every effort has been made to trace the copyright holders of referred material. Where these efforts have not been successful, copyright owners are invited to contact the Editor (Guidora) so that their copyright can be acknowledged and/or the material removed from the publication.

Creative Commons Content

We are most grateful to publishers of Creative Commons material, including images. Our policies concerning this material are (1) to credit the copyright owner, and provide a link where possible (2) to remove Creative Commons material, at once, if the copyright owner so requests - for example, if the owner changes the licensing of an image.

We will also keep our interpretation of the Creative Commons Non-Commercial license under review. Along with, we believe, most web publishers, our current view is that acceptance of the 'Non-Commercial' condition means (1) we must not sell the image or any publication containing the image (2) we may, however, use an image as an illustration for some information which is not being sold or offered for sale.

Note to other copyright owners

We are grateful to those copyright owners who have given permission for their material to be used. Some of the material comes from secondary and tertiary sources. In every case, we have tried to locate the original author or photographer and make the appropriate acknowledgment. In some cases, the sources have proved obscure, and we have been unable to track them down. In these cases, we would like to hear from the copyright owners and will be pleased to acknowledge them in future editions or remove the material.

Made in the USA
Las Vegas, NV
17 September 2024

95423798R00075